Workshop on Automatic Simultaneous Translation Challenges, Recent Advances, and Future Directions 2020

Online
10 July 2020

ISBN: 978-1-7138-1391-0

Printed from e-media with permission by:

Curran Associates, Inc.
57 Morehouse Lane
Red Hook, NY 12571

CURRAN ASSOCIATES INC. proceedings.com

Some format issues inherent in the e-media version may also appear in this print version.

Association for Computational Linguistics
209 N. Eighth Street
Stroudsburg, Pennsylvania 18360

Phone: 1-570-476-8006
Fax: 1-570-476-0860

acl@aclweb.org

Additional copies of this publication are available from:

Curran Associates, Inc.
57 Morehouse Lane
Red Hook, NY 12571 USA
Phone: 845-758-0400
Fax: 845-758-2633
Email: curran@proceedings.com
Web: www.proceedings.com

ACL 2020

Workshop on Automatic Simultaneous Translation Challenges, Recent Advances, and Future Directions

Proceedings of the Workshop

July, 10, 2020

Introduction

Welcome to the First Workshop on Automatic Simultaneous Translation (AutoSimTrans). Simultaneous translation, which performs translation concurrently with the source speech, is widely useful in many scenarios such as international conferences, negotiations, press releases, legal proceedings, and medicine. It combines the AI technologies of machine translation (MT), automatic speech recognition (ASR), and text-to-speech synthesis (TTS), and is becoming a cutting-edge research field.

As an emerging and interdisciplinary field, simultaneous translation faces many great challenges, and is considered one of the holy grails of AI. This workshop will bring together researchers and practitioners in machine translation, speech processing, and human interpretation, to discuss recent advances and open challenges of simultaneous translation.

We organized a simultaneous translation shared task on Chinese-English. We released a dataset for open research, which covers speeches in a wide range of domains, such as IT, economy, culture, biology, arts, etc.

We also have two sets of keynote speakers: Hua Wu, Colin Cherry, Jordan Boyd-Graber, Qun Liu from simultaneous translation, Kay-Fan Cheung and Barry Slaughter Olsen from human interpretation research. We hope this workshop will greatly increase the communication and crossfertilization between the two fields.

We look forward to an exciting workshop.

Hua Wu, Colin Cherry, Liang Huang, Zhongjun He, Mark Liberman, James Cross, Yang Liu

Organizers:

Hua Wu, Baidu Inc.
Colin Cherry, Google
Liang Huang, Oregon State University and Baidu Research
Zhongjun He, Baidu Inc.
Mark Liberman, University of Pennsylvania
James Cross, Facebook
Yang Liu, Tsinghua University

Program Committee:

Mingbo Ma, Baidu Research, USA
Naveen Arivazhagan, Google, USA
Chung-Cheng Chiu, Google, USA
Kenneth Church, Baidu Research, USA
Yang Feng, CAS/ICT, China
George Foster, Google, Canada
Alvin Grissom II, Ursinus College, USA
He He, NYU, USA
Alina Karakanta, FBK-Trento, Italy
Wei Li, Google, USA
Hairong Liu, Baidu Research, USA
Kaibo Liu, Baidu Research, USA
Wolfgang Macherey, Google, USA
Jan Niehues, Maastricht U., Netherlands
Yusuke Oda, Google, Japan
Colin Raffel, Google, USA
Elizabeth Salesky, CMU, USA
Jiajun Zhang, CAS/IA, China
Ruiqing Zhang, Baidu Inc. China
Renjie Zheng, Oregon State Univ., USA

Invited Speakers:

Hua Wu, Chief Scientist of NLP, Baidu Inc., China
Colin Cherry, Research Scientist in Google Translate, Google Inc., Montreal, Canada
Jordan Boyd-Graber, Associate Professor, University of Maryland, USA
Qun Liu, Chief Scientist of Speech and Language Computing, Huawei Noah's Ark Lab, China
Kay-Fan Cheung, Associate Professor, The Hong Kong Polytechnic University, Member of the International Association of Conference Interpreters (AIIC), China
Barry Slaughter Olsen, Professor, the Middlebury Institute of International Studies and Conference Interpreter, Member of AIIC, USA

Table of Contents

Conference Program

Friday, July 10, 2020

8:50–9:00 *Opening Remarks*

9:00–11:00 Session 1

9:00–9:30 *Invited Talk 1: Colin Cherry*

9:30–10:00 *Invited Talk 2: Barry Slaughter Olsen*

10:00–10:30 *Invited Talk 3: Jordan Boyd-Graber*

10:30–11:00 *Q&A*

11:00–14:00 Lunch

17:00–19:00 Session 2

17:00–17:30 *Invited Talk 4: Hua Wu*

17:30–18:00 *Invited Talk 5: Kay-Fan Cheung*

18:00–18:30 *Invited Talk 6: Qun Liu*

18:30–19:00 *Q&A*

Friday, July 10, 2020 (continued)

19:00–19:30 Break

19:30–21:00 Session 3: Research Paper and System Description

19:30–19:40 *Dynamic Sentence Boundary Detection for Simultaneous Translation*
Ruiqing Zhang and Chuanqiang Zhang

19:40–19:50 *End-to-End Speech Translation with Adversarial Training*
Xuancai Li, Chen Kehai, Tiejun Zhao and Muyun Yang

19:50–20:00 *Robust Neural Machine Translation with ASR Errors*
Haiyang Xue, Yang Feng, Shuhao Gu and Wei Chen

20:00–20:10 *Improving Autoregressive NMT with Non-Autoregressive Model*
Long Zhou, Jiajun Zhang and Chengqing Zong

20:10–20:20 *Modeling Discourse Structure for Document-level Neural Machine Translation*
Junxuan Chen, Xiang Li, Jiarui Zhang, Chulun Zhou, Jianwei Cui, Bin Wang and Jinsong Su

20:20–20:30 *BIT's system for the AutoSimTrans 2020*
Minqin Li, Haodong Cheng, Yuanjie Wang, Sijia Zhang, Liting Wu and Yuhang Guo

20:30–21:00 *Q&A*

21:00–21:10 *Closing Remarks*

Dynamic Sentence Boundary Detection for Simultaneous Translation

Ruiqing Zhang
Baidu, Inc., / Beijing, China
zhangruiqing01@baidu.com

Chuanqiang Zhang
Baidu, Inc., / Beijing, China
zhangchuanqiang@baidu.com

Abstract

Simultaneous Translation is a great challenge in which translation starts before the source sentence finished. Most studies take transcription as input and focus on balancing translation quality and latency for each sentence. However, most ASR systems can not provide accurate sentence boundaries in realtime. Thus it is a key problem to segment sentences for the word streaming before translation. In this paper, we propose a novel method for sentence boundary detection that takes it as a multi-class classification task under the end-to-end pre-training framework. Experiments show significant improvements both in terms of translation quality and latency.

1 Introduction

Simultaneous Translation aims to translate the speech of a source language into a target language as quickly as possible without interrupting the speaker. Typically, a simultaneous translation system is comprised of an auto-speech-recognition (ASR) model and a machine translation (MT) model. The ASR model transforms the audio signal into the text of source language and the MT model translates the source text into the target language.

Recent studies on simultaneous translation (Cho and Esipova, 2016; Ma et al., 2019; Arivazhagan et al., 2019) focus on the trade-off between translation quality and latency. They explore a policy that determines when to begin translating with the input of a stream of transcription. However, there is a gap between transcription and ASR that some ASR model doesn't provide punctuations or cannot provide accurate punctuation in realtime, while the transcription is always well-formed. See Figure 1 for illustration. Without sentence boundaries, the state-of-the-art *wait-k* model takes insufficient text as input and produces an incorrect translation.

Therefore, sentence boundary detection (or sentence segmentation) [1] plays an important role to narrow the gap between the ASR and transcription. A good segmentation will not only improve translation quality but also reduce latency.

Studies of sentence segmentation falls into one of the following two bins:

- The strategy performs segmentation from a speech perspective. Fügen et al. (2007) and Bangalore et al. (2012) used prosodic pauses in speech recognition as segmentation boundaries. This method is effective in dialogue scenarios, with clear silence during the conversation. However, it does not work well in long speech audio, such as lecture scenarios. According to Venuti (2012), silence-based chunking accounts for only 6.6%, 10%, and 17.1% in English, French, and German, respectively. Indicating that in most cases, it cannot effectively detect boundaries for streaming words.

- The strategy takes segmentation as a standard text processing problem. The studies considered the problem as classification or sequence labeling, based on SVM, (Sridhar et al., 2013) conditional random filed (CRFs) (Lu and Ng, 2010; Wang et al., 2012; Ueffing et al., 2013). Other researches utilized language model, either based on N-gram (Wang et al., 2016) or recurrent neural network (RNN)(Tilk and Alumäe, 2015).

In this paper, we use classification to solve the problem of sentence segmentation from the perspective of text. Instead of predicting a sentence boundary for a certain position, we propose a multi-position boundary prediction approach. Specifically, for a source text $\mathbf{x} = \{x_1, ..., x_T\}$, we calculate the probability of predicting sentence boundary

[1] We use both terms interchangeably in this paper.

Proceedings of the 1st Workshop on Automatic Simultaneous Translation, pages 1–9

src	One	of	two	things	is	going	to	happen	.	Either	**it**	**'s**	**going**	**to**	...
Reference	Eines von zwei Dingen wird passieren.									Entweder **wird** ...					
wait3				Eines	von	zwei	Dingen	wird	passieren.				Entweder	**wird**	...
src without boundary	One	of	two	things	is	going	to	happen	either	**it**	**'s**	**going**	**to**	...	
wait3				Eines	von	zwei	Dingen	wird	passieren	entweder	es	ist	geht	dass	...

Figure 1: An English-to-German example that translates from a streaming source with and without sentence boundaries. We take the wait-K model (Ma et al., 2019) for illustration, K=3 here. The *wait3* model first performs three READ (wait) action at the beginning of each sentence (as shown in blue), and then alternating one READ with one WRITE action in the following steps. Given the input source without sentence boundaries (in the $4^{th} line$), the *wait3* model (in the $5^{th} line$) doesn't take the three READ action at the beginning of following sentences. Therefore, the English phrase "it's going to", which should have been translated as "wird", produced a meaningless translation "es ist geht dass" with limited context during *wait3* model inference.

after x_t , $t = T, T-1, ..., T-M$. Thus the latency of translation can be controlled within $L+M$ words, where L is the length of the sentence. Inspired by the recent pre-training techniques (Devlin et al., 2019; Sun et al., 2019) that successfully used in many NLP tasks, we used a pre-trained model for initialization and fine-tune the model on the source side of the sentence. Overall, the contributions are as follows:

- We propose a novel sentence segmentation method based on pre-trained language representations, which have been successfully used in various NLP tasks.
- Our method dynamically predicts the boundary at multiple locations, rather than a specific location, achieving high accuracy with low latency.

2 Background

Recent studies show that the pre-training and fine-tuning framework achieves significant improvements in various NLP tasks. Generally, a model is first pre-trained on large unlabeled data. After that, on the fine-tuning step, the model is initialized by the parameters obtained by the pre-training step and fine-tuned using labeled data for specific tasks.

Devlin et al. (2019) proposed a generalized framework BERT, to learn language representations based on a deep Transformer (Vaswani et al., 2017) encoder. Rather than traditionally train a language model from-left-to-right or from-right-to-left, they proposed a masked language model (MLM) that randomly replace some tokens in a sequence by a placeholder (mask) and trained the model to predict the original tokens. They also pre-train the model for the next sentence prediction (NSP) task that is to predict whether a sentence is the subsequent sentence of the first sentence. Sun et al. (2019) proposed a pre-training framework ERNIE, by integrating more knowledge. Rather than masking single tokens, they proposed to mask a group of words on different levels, such as entities, phrases, etc. The model achieves state-of-the-art performances on many NLP tasks.

In this paper, we train our model under the ERNIE framework.

3 Our Method

Given a streaming input $\mathbf{x} = \{x_1, ..., x_t, ..., x_T\}$, the task of sentence segmentation is to determine whether $x_t \in \mathbf{x}$ is the end of a sentence. Thus the task can be considered as a classification problem, that is $p(y_t|\mathbf{x}, \theta)$, where $y_t \in \{0, 1\}$. However, in simultaneous translation scenario, the latency is unacceptable if we take the full source text as contextual information. Thus we should limit the context size and make a decision dynamically.

As the input is a word streaming, the sentence boundary detection problem can be transformed as, whether there exists a sentence boundary until the current word x_t. Thus we can use the word streaming as a context to make a prediction. We propose a multi-class classification model to predict the probability of a few words before x_t as sentence boundaries (Section 3.1). We use the ERNIE framework to first pre-train a language representation and then fine-tune it to sentence boundary detection (Section 3.2). We also propose a dynamic voted inference strategy (Section 3.3).

3.1 The Model

For a streaming input $\mathbf{x} = \{x_1, ..., x_t\}$, our goal is to detect whether there is a sentence boundary

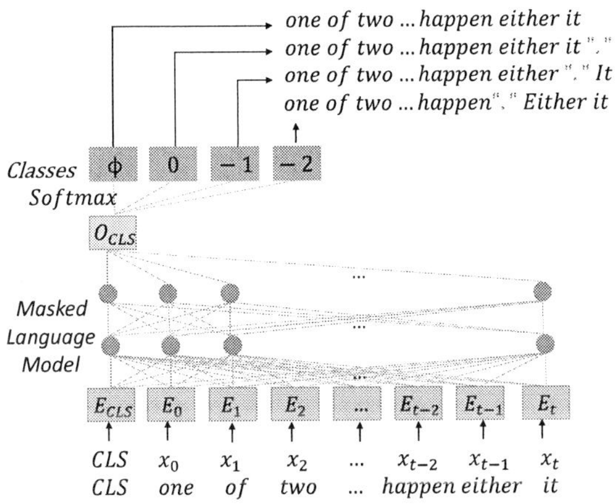

Figure 2: Illustration of the dynamic classification model. $M = 2$ means there are 4 classes. We use ERNIE to train a classifier. Class ϕ means that there is no sentence boundary in the stream till now. Class $-m$ $m = 0, 1, 2$ means that x_{t-m} is the end of a sentence and we then put a period after it.

till the current word x_t from last sentence boundary. Rather than a binary classification that detects whether x_t is a sentence boundary, we propose a multi-class method. The classes are as follows:

$$y = \begin{cases} \phi, & \text{no sentence boundary detected} \\ 0, & x_t \quad \text{is the end of a sentence} \\ -1, & x_{t-1} \quad \text{is the end of a sentence} \\ \dots & \\ -M, & x_{t-M} \quad \text{is the end of a sentence} \end{cases}$$

where M is the maximum offset size to the current state. Thus, we have $M + 2$ classes.

See Figure 2 for illustration. We set $M = 2$, indicating that the model predicts 4 classes for the input stream. If the output class is ϕ, meaning that the model does not detect any sentence boundary. Thus the model will continue receiving new words. If the output class is 0, indicating that the current word x_t is the end of a sentence and we put a period after the word. Similarly, class $-m$ denotes to add a sentence boundary after x_{t-m}. While a sentence boundary is detected, the sentence will be extracted from the stream and sent to the MT system as an input for translation. The sentence detection then continues from x_{t-m+1}.

Each time our system receives a new word x_t, the classifier predicts probabilities for the last $M+1$ words as sentence boundaries. If the output class is ϕ, the classifier receives a new word x_{t+1}, and recompute the probabilities for $x_{t+1}, x_t, x_{t-1}, \dots, x_{t-M+1}$. Generally, more contextual information will help the classifier improve the precision (Section 4.5).

3.2 Training Objective

Our training data is extracted from paragraphs. Question marks, exclamation marks, and semicolons are mapped to periods and all other punctuation symbols are removed from the corpora. Then for every two adjacent sentences in a paragraph, we concatenate them to form a long sequence, $\mathbf{x}$. We record the position of the period as r and then remove the period from the sequence.

For $x = (x_1, x_2, \dots, x_N)$ with N words, we generate $r + M$ samples for $t = 1, 2, \dots, (r + M)$, in the form of $< (x_1, \dots, x_t), y_t >$, where y_t is the label that:

$$y_t = \left\{ \begin{array}{ll} \phi, & \text{if} \quad t < r \\ -(t-r), & \text{if} \quad t \in [r, r+M] \end{array} \right\} \quad (1)$$

Note that if the length of the second sentence is less than M, we concatenate subsequent sentences until $r + M$ samples are collected. Then we define the loss function as follows:

$$\begin{aligned} \mathcal{J}(\theta) = \sum_{(\mathbf{x},r)\in D} & log(\sum_{t=1}^{r-1} p(y_t = \phi | x_{\leq t}; \theta) \\ & + \sum_{t=r}^{r+M} p(y_t = -(t-r)) | x_{\leq t}; \theta)) \end{aligned} \quad (2)$$

where D is the dataset that contains pairs of concatenated sentences $\mathbf{x}$ and its corresponding position of the removed periods r. M is a hyperparameter denotes the number of waiting words.

Note that our method differs from previous work in the manner of classification. Sridhar et al. (2013) predicts whether a word x_t labeled as the end of a sentence or not by a binary classification:

$$p(y_t = 0 | x_{t-2}^{t+2}) + p(y_t = 1 | x_{t-2}^{t+2}) = 1 \quad (3)$$

where $y_t = 0$ means x_t is not the end of a sentence and $y_t = 1$ means x_t is the end. x_{t-2}^{t+2} denotes 5 words $x_{t-2}, x_{t-1}, \dots, x_{t+2}$.

Some other language-model based work (Wang et al., 2016) calculates probabilities over all words in the vocabulary including the period:

$$\sum_{w \in V \cup \text{"."}} p(y_t = w | x_{\leq t}) = 1 \quad (4)$$

and decides whether x_t is a sentence boundary by comparing the probability of $y_t =$"." and $y_t = x_{t+1}$.

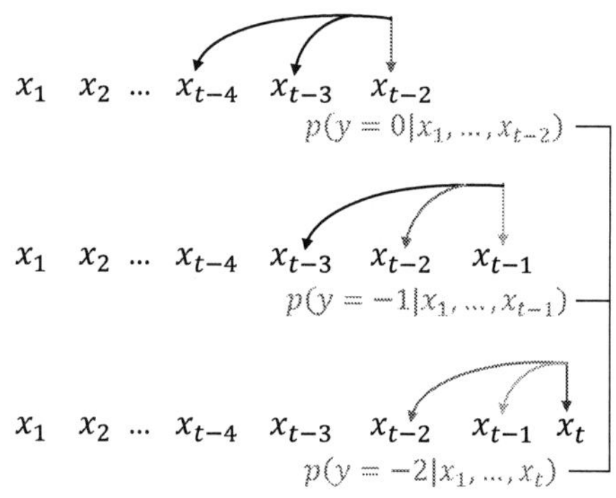

Figure 3: Our voting algorithm for online prediction with M equals to 2. Input the stream text till x_t, the overall probability of add a sentence boundary after x_{t-2} is averaged by the $M+1$ probabilities in red, while for x_{t-1} (in green) and x_t (in blue), the number of deterministic probability is less than $M+1$.

The performance of these methods is limited by incomplete semantics, without considering global boundary detection. In our methods, we leverage more future words and restrict classes globally:

$$p(y_t = \phi|x_{\leq t}) + \sum_{m=0}^{M} p(y_t = -m|x_{\leq t}) = 1 \quad (5)$$

The restriction is motivated that in a lecture scenario, where a sentence could not be very short that contains only 1 or 2 words. Thus, the probability distribution prohibits that adjacent words to be the end of sentences at the same time.

3.3 Dynamic Inference

At inference time, we predict sentence boundaries sequentially with a dynamic voting strategy. Each time a new word x_t is received, we predict the probability of $M+1$ classes as shown in the bottom of Figure 3, then calculate if the probability of previous $M+1$ positions $(x_{t-M}, x_{t-M+1}, x_t)$ is larger then a threshold θ_{Th}. If yes, we add a sentence boundary at the corresponding position. Otherwise, we continue to receive new words.

Note that the probability is adopted as the voted probability. While the probability of adding a sentence boundary after x_{t-M} has $M+1$ probabilities to calculate the average, the number of probabilities to determine whether it is a sentence boundary at subsequent positions is less than $M+1$. Here we use the voted average of existing probabilities. Specifically, to judge whether $x_{t'}$ is a sentence boundary, it needs $t-t'+1$ probabilities:

$$\frac{1}{t-t'+1}\sum_{m=0}^{t-t'} p(y=-m|x_1,...,x_{t+m}) \quad (6)$$

where $t' \in [t-M, t]$.

If more than one sentence boundary probabilities for $x_{t-M},...,x_t$ exceeds the threshold θ_{Th} at the same time, we choose the front-most position as a sentence boundary. This is consistent with our training process, that is, if there is a sample of two or more sentence boundaries, we ignore the following and label the class y_t according to the first boundary. This is because we generate samples with each period in the original paragraph as depicted in Section 3.2. From another point of view, the strategy can also compensate for some incorrect suppression of adjacent boundaries, thereby improving online prediction accuracy.

	Dataset	Sentences	Tokens/s
Train	WMT 14	4.4M	23.22
	IWSLT 14	0.19M	20.26
Test	IWSLT 2010-2014	7040	19.03

Table 1: Experimental Corpora without punctuation. Token/s denotes the number of tokens per sentence in English.

4 Experiment

Experiments are conducted on English-German (En-De) simultaneous translation. We evaluate 1) the F-score[2] of sentence boundary detection and 2) case-sensitive tokenized 4-gram BLEU (Papineni et al., 2002) as the final translation effect of the segmented sentences. To reduce the impact of the ASR system, we use the transcription without punctuation in both training and evaluation.

The datasets used in our experiments are listed in Table 1. We use two parallel corpus from machine translation task: WMT 14[3] and IWSLT 14 [4]. WMT 14 is a text translation corpus including 4.4M sentences, mainly on news and web sources. And IWSLT 14 is a speech translation corpus of TED lectures with transcribed text and corresponding translation. Here we only use the text part in it, containing 0.19M sentences in the training set.

[2]harmonic average of the precision and recall
[3]http://www.statmt.org/wmt14/translation-task.html
[4]https://wit3.fbk.eu/

Method	Hyperparameter	F-score	BLEU	avgCW	maxCW
Oracle	NA	1.0	22.76	NA	NA
N-gram	N=5, $\theta_{Th} = e^{0.0}$	0.46	17.83	**6.64**	56
N-gram	N=5, $\theta_{Th} = e^{2.0}$	0.48	19.20	13.43	161
T-LSTM	d=256	0.55	20.46	10.14	53
dynamic-force	$\theta_l = 40, \theta_{Th} = 0.5$	**0.74**	**22.01**	14.43	**40**
dynamic-base	$\theta_{Th} = 0.5$	**0.74**	21.93	14.58	50

Table 2: Segmentation Performance trained on IWSLT2014. All methods are conducted with future words M equals to 1.

We train the machine translation model on WMT 14 with the base version of the Transformer model (Vaswani et al., 2017), achieving a BLEU score of 27.2 on newstest2014. And our sentence boundary detection model is trained on the source transcription of IWSLT 14 unless otherwise specified (Section 4.3). To evaluate the system performance, we merge the IWSLT test set of 4 years (2010-2014) to construct a big test set of 7040 sentences. The overall statistics of our dataset is shown in Table 1.

We evaluate our model and two existing methods listed below:

- *dynamic-base* is our proposed method that detect sentence boundaries dynamically using a multi-class classification.
- *dynamic-force* adds a constraint on *dynamic-base*. In order to keep in line with (Wang et al., 2016), we add a constraint that sentence should be force segmented if longer than θ_l.
- *N-gram* is the method using an N-gram language model to compare the probability of adding vs. not adding a boundary at x_t after receiving $x_{t-N+1}, ..., x_t$. We implement according to (Wang et al., 2016).
- *T-LSTM* uses a RNN-based classification model with two classes. We implement a unidirectional RNN and perform training according to (Tilk and Alumäe, 2015)[5].

Our classifier in *dynamic-base* and *dynamic-force* is trained under ERNIE base framework. We use the released [6] parameters obtained at pretraining step as initialization. In the fine-tuning stage, we use a learning rate of $2e^{-5}$.

[5] we only keep the two classes of *period* and ϕ in this work

[6] https://github.com/PaddlePaddle/ERNIE

4.1 Overall Results

Table 2 reports the results of source sentence segmentation on En-De translation, where the latency is measured by Consecutive Wait (CW) (Gu et al., 2017), the number of words between two translate actions. To eliminate the impact of the different policies in simultaneous translation, we only execute translation at the end of each sentence. Therefore, the CW here denotes the sentence length L plus the number of future words M. We calculate its average and maximum value as "avgCW" and "maxCW", respectively. Better performance expect high F-score, BLEU, and low latency (CW). The translation effect obtained by using the groundtruth period as the sentence segmentation is shown in the first line of *Oracle*.

The *N-gram* method calculate the probability of add (p_{add}) and not add (p_{not}) period at each position, and decide whether to chunk by comparing whether p_{add}/p_{not} exceeds θ_{Th}. The N-gram method without threshold tuning (with $\theta_{Th} = e^{0.0}$) divides sentences into small pieces, achieving the lowest average latency of 6.64. However, the F-score of segmentation is very low because of the incomplete essence of the n-gram feature. Notable, the precision and recall differs much ($precision = 0.33, recall = 0.78$) in this setup. Therefore, we need to choose a better threshold by grid search (Wang et al., 2016). With θ_{Th} equals to $e^{2.0}$, the F-score of N-gram method increased a little bit ($0.46 \rightarrow 0.48$), with a more balanced precision and recall ($precision = 0.51, recall = 0.48$). However, the max latency runs out of control, resulting in a maximum of 161 words in a sentence. We also tried to shorten the latency of the N-gram method by force segmentation (Wang et al., 2016), but the result was very poor ($precision = 0.33, recall = 0.40$).

The *T-LSTM* method with the hidden size of 256 performs better than *N-gram*, but the F-score

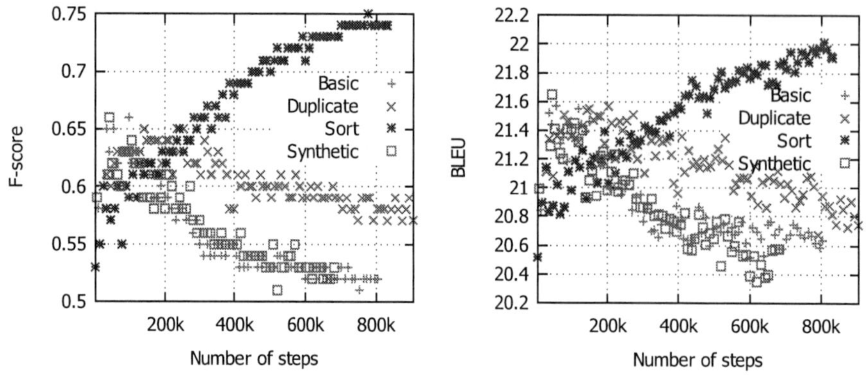

Figure 4: Performance evaluated on IWSLT14 testset for different training sample building strategies.

and BLEU is still limited. On the contrary, our *dynamic*-based approaches with $M = 1$ achieve the best F-score at 0.74 and the final translation is very close to the result of *Oracle*. In particular, the precision and recall reached about 0.72 and 0.77 in both *dynamic-force* and *dynamic-base*, respectively. Accurate sentence segmentation brings better performance in translation, bringing an improvement of 1.55 over *T-LSTM*. Moreover, our approach is not inferior in terms of latency. Both average latency and max latency is controlled at a relatively low level.

It is interesting to note that, *dynamic-force* performs better than *dynamic-base*, in terms of latency and BLEU. This suggests the effectiveness of the force segmentation strategy, that is, select the chunking location with a sentence length limitation will not affect the accuracy of segmentation, and would enhance the translation effect.

4.2 Magic in Data Processing

According to Section 3.2, the order between sentences of original corpora would affect the generation of training samples. In this section, we investigate the effect of various data reordering strategies.

A basic method is to use the original sentence order of speech corpora, denote as ***Basic***. However, the samples generated is limited, which makes the model easy to over-fit. To overcome this problem, we adopt two methods to expand data scale: 1) ***Duplicate*** the original data multiple times or 2) Add ***Synthetic*** adjacent sentences, through randomly selecting two sentences from the corpora. These two methods greatly expand the total amount of data, but the gain to the model is uncertain. As an alternative, we explore a ***Sort*** method, to sort sentences according to alphabetic order.

The performance of the four training data organization methods is shown in Figure 4, all built on IWSLT2014 and conducted under the setup of $M = 1$ and $\theta_l = 40$. It is clear that *Basic*, *Duplicate* and *Synthetic* are all involved in the problem of over-fitting. They quickly achieved their best results and then gradually declined. Surprisingly, the *Sort* approach is prominent in both segmentation accuracy and translation performance. This may be due to the following reasons: 1) Sentence classification is not a difficult task, especially when $M = 1$ for 3-class classification ($y \in [\phi, 0, -1]$), making the task easy to over-fit. 2) Compared with *Basic*, *Duplicate* is more abundant in the sample combination in batch training, but there is no essential difference between the two methods. 3) *Synthetic* hardly profits our model, because the synthesized data may be very simple due to random selection. 4) *Sort* may simulate difficult cases in real scenes and train them pertinently, bringing it a poor performance at start but not prone to overfit. There are many samples with identical head and tail words in the sorted data, such as: "*and it gives me a lot of hope* || *and ...*" and "*that means there's literally thousands of new ideas* || *that ...* ". Even human beings find it difficult to determine whether the words before || is sentence boundaries of these samples. In *Basic*, *Duplicate* and *Synthetic* methods, such samples are usually submerged in a large quantity of simple samples. However, the data organization mode of *Sort* greatly strengthens the model's ability to learn these difficult samples.

There is no need to worry that the *Sort* method cannot cover simple samples. Because we sort by rows in source file, and some of the rows contain multiple sentences (an average of 1.01 sentences

Method	F-score	BLEU	avgCW	maxCW
N-gram	0.48	19.58	15.60	156
T-LSTM	0.56	20.77	15.65	51
dyn-force	**0.68**	**21.48**	**15.53**	**40**
dyn-base	**0.68**	21.40	16.08	46

Table 3: Segmentation Performance trained on WMT14. All methods are conducted with future words M equals to 1. *N-gram* uses grid-search to get the best hyperparamters. *dyn* is short for *dynamic* and *dynamic-force* adopts $\theta_l = 40$.

θ_l	F-score	BLEU	avgCW
10	0.40	16.27	**5.85**
20	0.58	20.34	9.74
40	**0.74**	**22.01**	14.43
80	0.73	21.60	15.15

Table 4: Segmentation Performance of *dynamic-force* trained on IWSLT2014. All methods are conducted with future words M equals to 1.

per row), which are in real speech order. We argue that these sentences are sufficient to model the classification of simple samples, based on the rapid overfit performance of the other three methods.

4.3 Out-of-Domain vs. In-Domain

Next, we turn to the question that how does the domain of training corpus affects results. With the test set unchanged, we compare the sentence boundary detections model trained on out-of-domain corpora WMT 14 and in-domain corpora IWSLT 14, respectively.

As mentioned before, WMT 14 is a larger text translation corpus mainly on news and web sources. But the test set comes from IWSLT, which contains transcriptions of TED lectures of various directions. Intuitively, larger dataset provides more diverse samples, but due to domain changes, it does not necessarily lead to improvements in accuracy.

The performance of various models trained on WMT14 is shown in Table 3. *Dynamic-force* also achieves the best translation performance with a relatively small latency on average and limited the max latency within 40 words. However, it underperforms the same model trained on IWSLT2014 (as shown in Table 2), demonstrating its sensitivity to the training domain.

On the contrary, *N-gram* and *T-LSTM* is hardly affected. For *N-gram*, one possible reason is the before mentioned weakness of the N-gram: segmentation depends on only N previous words, which is more steady compared to the whole sentence, thus eliminating the perturbation of whole sentence brought by the domain variation. For *T-LSTM*, it even improves a little compared with its in-domain performance. This may be due to the lack of training samples. 0.19M sentences of IWSLT2014 is insufficient to fit the parameters of *T-LSTM*. Thus the model would benefit from increasing the corpus size. However, our method needs less data in training because our model has been pre-trained. Based on a powerful representation, we need only a small amount of training data in fine-tuning, which is best aligned with the test set in the domain.

4.4 Length of window θ_l

Next, we discuss the effect of changing θ. The performance of *dynamic-force* with varying θ_l is shown in Table 4. Smaller θ_l brings shorter latency, as well as worse performance. The effect is extremely poor with $\theta_l = 10$. There are two possible reasons: 1) Constraint sentence length less than θ_l is too harsh under small θ_l, 2) The discrepancy between the unrestricted training and length-restricted testing causes the poor effect.

We first focus on the second possible reason. While the difference between *dynamic-base* and *dynamic-force* is only in prediction, we want to know whether we can achieve better results by controlling the length of training samples. Accordingly, we only use the samples shorter than a fixed value: θ_l in training phrase. At inference time, we use both *dynamic-force* with the same sentence length constraint θ_l and *dynamic-base* to predict sentence boundaries. As elaborated in Figure 5, For each pair of curves with a same θ_l, *dynamic-force* and *dynamic-base* present similar performance. This demonstrates the main reason for the poor performance with small θ_l is not the training-testing discrepancy but lies in the first reason that the force constraint is too harsh.

Moreover, it is interesting to find that the performance of $\theta_l = 80$ is similar with $\theta_l = 40$ at the beginning but falls a little during training. This probably because the setup with $\theta_l = 40$ can filter some inaccurate cases, as the average number of words in IWSLT2014 training set is 20.26.

4.5 Number of Future Words M

We investigate whether can we achieve better performance with more or less future words. We experiment with M from 0 to 5. The result is shown

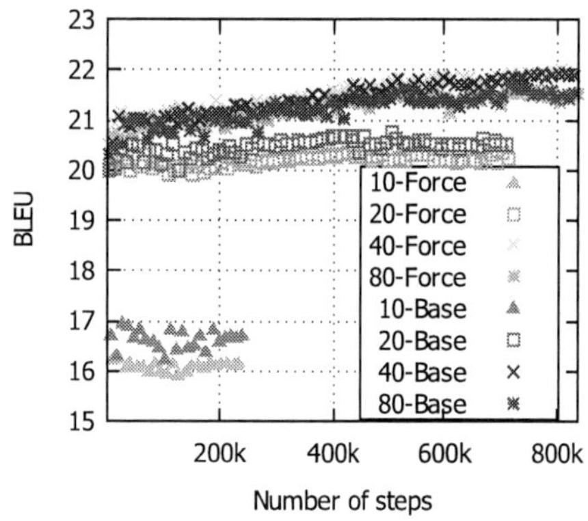

Figure 5: Translation performance on IWSLT2014 test-set. "θ_l-Force" denotes to set the sentence length threshold to θ_l in both training sample generation and prediction. "θ_l-Base" is to set this constraint only in training samples generation process.

M	F-score	BLEU	avgCW
0	0.66	21.54	13.23
1	0.74	22.01	14.43
2	0.77	22.23	15.24
3	0.79	22.23	16.52
4	0.80	22.29	17.15

Table 5: Segmentation Performance of *dynamic-force* trained on IWSLT2014. All methods are conducted with $\theta_l = 40$.

in Table 5. Reducing M to zero means that do not refer to any future words in prediction. This degrades performance a lot, proving the effectiveness of adding future words in prediction. Increase M from 1 to 2 also promote the performance in both sentence boundary detection f-score and the system BLEU. However, as more future words added (increase M to 3 and 4), the improvement becomes less obvious.

5 Related Work

Sentence boundary detection has been explored for years, but the majority of these work focuses on offline punctuation restoration, instead of applied in simultaneous translation. Existing work can be divided into two classes according to the model input.

5.1 N-gram based methods

Some work takes a fixed size of words as input. Focus on utilizing a limited size of the streaming input, they predict the probability of putting a boundary at a specific position x_t by a N-gram language model (Wang et al., 2016) or a classification model (Sridhar et al., 2013; Yarmohammadi et al., 2013). The language-model based method make decision depends on N words ($x_{t-N+2}, ..., x_{t+1}$) and compares its probability with ($x_{t-N+2}, ..., x_t$,"."). The classification model takes features of N words around x_t and classifies to two classes denoting x_t is a sentence boundary or not. The main deficiency of this method is that the dependencies outside the input window are lost, resulting in low accuracy.

5.2 Whole sentence-based methods

Some other work focuses on restoring punctuation and capitalization using the whole sentence. To improve the sentence boundary classification accuracy, some work upgrade the N-gram input to variable-length input by using recurrent neural network (RNN) (Tilk and Alumäe, 2015; Salloum et al., 2017). Some other work takes punctuation restoration as a sequence labeling problem and investigates using Conditional Random Fields (CRFs) (Lu and Ng, 2010; Wang et al., 2012; Ueffing et al., 2013). Peitz et al. (2011) and Cho et al. (2012) treats this problem as a machine translation task, training to translate non-punctuated transcription into punctuated text. However, all these methods utilize the whole sentence information, which is not fit for the simultaneous translation scenario. Moreover, the translation model based methods require multiple steps of decoding, making it unsuitable for online prediction.

6 Conclusion

In this paper, we propose an online sentence boundary detection approach. With the input of streaming words, our model predicts the probability of multiple positions rather than a certain position. By adding this adjacent position constraint and using dynamic prediction, our method achieves higher accuracy with lower latency.

We also incorporate the pre-trained technique, ERNIE to implement our classification model. The empirical results on IWSLT2014 demonstrate that our approach achieves significant improvements of 0.19 F-score on sentence segmentation and 1.55 BLEU points compared with the language-model based methods.

References

Naveen Arivazhagan, Colin Cherry, Wolfgang Macherey, Chung-Cheng Chiu, Semih Yavuz,

Ruoming Pang, Wei Li, and Colin Raffel. 2019. Monotonic infinite lookback attention for simultaneous machine translation. In *Proceedings of the 57th Annual Meeting of the Association for Computational Linguistics*. Association for Computational Linguistics.

Srinivas Bangalore, Vivek Kumar Rangarajan Sridhar, Prakash Kolan, Ladan Golipour, and Aura Jimenez. 2012. Real-time incremental speech-to-speech translation of dialogs. In *Proceedings of the 2012 Conference of the North American Chapter of the Association for Computational Linguistics: Human Language Technologies*. Association for Computational Linguistics.

Eunah Cho, Jan Niehues, and Alex Waibel. 2012. Segmentation and punctuation prediction in speech language translation using a monolingual translation system. In *International Workshop on Spoken Language Translation (IWSLT) 2012*.

Kyunghyun Cho and Masha Esipova. 2016. Can neural machine translation do simultaneous translation? *arXiv preprint arXiv:1606.02012*.

Jacob Devlin, Ming-Wei Chang, Kenton Lee, and Kristina Toutanova. 2019. Bert: Pre-training of deep bidirectional transformers for language understanding. In *Proceedings of NAACL-HLT 2019*.

Christian Fügen, Alex Waibel, and Muntsin Kolss. 2007. Simultaneous translation of lectures and speeches. *Machine translation*, 21(4).

Jiatao Gu, Graham Neubig, Kyunghyun Cho, and Victor OK Li. 2017. Learning to translate in real-time with neural machine translation.

Wei Lu and Hwee Tou Ng. 2010. Better punctuation prediction with dynamic conditional random fields. In *Proceedings of the 2010 conference on empirical methods in natural language processing*.

Mingbo Ma, Liang Huang, Hao Xiong, Kaibo Liu, Chuanqiang Zhang, Zhongjun He, Hairong Liu, Xing Li, and Haifeng Wang. 2019. STACL: simultaneous translation with integrated anticipation and controllable latency. In *Proceedings of the 57th Annual Meeting of the Association for Computational Linguistics*.

Kishore Papineni, Salim Roukos, Todd Ward, and Wei-Jing Zhu. 2002. Bleu: a method for automatic evaluation of machine translation. In *Proceedings of the 40th annual meeting on association for computational linguistics*. Association for Computational Linguistics.

Stephan Peitz, Markus Freitag, Arne Mauser, and Hermann Ney. 2011. Modeling punctuation prediction as machine translation. In *International Workshop on Spoken Language Translation (IWSLT) 2011*.

Wael Salloum, Gregory Finley, Erik Edwards, Mark Miller, and David Suendermann-Oeft. 2017. Deep learning for punctuation restoration in medical reports. In *BioNLP 2017*.

Vivek Kumar Rangarajan Sridhar, John Chen, Srinivas Bangalore, Andrej Ljolje, and Rathinavelu Chengalvarayan. 2013. Segmentation strategies for streaming speech translation. In *Proceedings of the 2013 Conference of the North American Chapter of the Association for Computational Linguistics: Human Language Technologies*.

Yu Sun, Shuohuan Wang, Yukun Li, Shikun Feng, Xuyi Chen, Han Zhang, Xin Tian, Danxiang Zhu, Hao Tian, and Hua Wu. 2019. Ernie: Enhanced representation through knowledge integration. *arXiv preprint arXiv:1904.09223*.

Ottokar Tilk and Tanel Alumäe. 2015. Lstm for punctuation restoration in speech transcripts. In *Sixteenth annual conference of the international speech communication association*.

Nicola Ueffing, Maximilian Bisani, and Paul Vozila. 2013. Improved models for automatic punctuation prediction for spoken and written text. In *Interspeech*.

Ashish Vaswani, Noam Shazeer, Niki Parmar, Jakob Uszkoreit, Llion Jones, Aidan N Gomez, Łukasz Kaiser, and Illia Polosukhin. 2017. Attention is all you need. In *31st Conference on Neural Information Processing Systems (NIPS 2017)*.

L. Venuti. 2012. The translation studies reader.

Xiaolin Wang, Andrew Finch, Masao Utiyama, and Eiichiro Sumita. 2016. An efficient and effective online sentence segmenter for simultaneous interpretation. In *Proceedings of the 3rd Workshop on Asian Translation (WAT2016)*.

Xuancong Wang, Hwee Tou Ng, and Khe Chai Sim. 2012. Dynamic conditional random fields for joint sentence boundary and punctuation prediction. In *Thirteenth Annual Conference of the International Speech Communication Association*.

Mahsa Yarmohammadi, Vivek Kumar Rangarajan Sridhar, Srinivas Bangalore, and Baskaran Sankaran. 2013. Incremental segmentation and decoding strategies for simultaneous translation. In *Proceedings of the Sixth International Joint Conference on Natural Language Processing*.

End-to-End Speech Translation with Adversarial Training

Xuancai Li[1], Kehai Chen[2], Tiejun Zhao[1] and Muyun Yang[1]
[1] Harbin Institute of Technology, Harbin, China
[2]National Institute of Information and Communications Technology, Kyoto, Japan
xcli@hit-mtlab.net, khchen@nict.go.jp, {tjzhao, yangmuyun}@hit.edu.cn

Abstract

End-to-end speech translation usually leverages audio-to-text parallel data to train an available speech translation model which has shown impressive results on various speech translation tasks. Due to the artificial cost of collecting audio-to-text parallel data, the speech translation is a natural low-resource translation scenario, which greatly hinders its improvement. In this paper, we proposed a new adversarial training method to leverage target monolingual data to relieve the low-resource shortcoming of speech translation. In our method, the existing speech translation model is considered as a Generator to gain a target language output, and another neural Discriminator is used to guide the distinction between outputs of speech translation model and true target monolingual sentences. Experimental results on the CCMT 2019-BSTC dataset speech translation task demonstrate that the proposed methods can significantly improve the performance of the end-to-end speech translation.

1 Introduction

Typically, a traditional speech translation (ST) system usually consists of two components: an automatic speech recognition (ASR) model and a machine translation (MT) model. Firstly, the speech recognition module transcribes the source language speech into the source language utterances (Chan et al., 2016; Chiu et al., 2018). Secondly, the machine translation module translates the source language utterances into the target language utterances (Bahdanau et al., 2014). Due to the success of end-to-end approaches in both automatic speech recognition and machine translation, researchers are increasingly interested in end-to-end speech translation. And, it has shown impressive results on various speech translation tasks (Duong et al., 2016; Bérard et al., 2016, 2018).

However, due to the artificial cost of collecting audio-to-text parallel data, speech translation is a natural low-resource translation scenario, which greatly hinders its improvement. Actually, the audio-to-text parallel data has only tens to hundreds of hours which are equivalent to about hundreds of thousands of bilingual sentence pairs. Thus, it is far from enough for the training of a high-quality speech translation system compare to bilingual parallel data of millions or even tens of millions for training a high-quality text-only NMT. Recently, there have some recent works that explore to address this issue. Bansal et al. (2018) pre-trained an ASR model on high-resource data, and then fine-tuned the ASR model for low-resource scenarios. Weiss et al. (2017) and Anastasopoulos and Chiang (2018) proposed multi-task learning methods to train the ST model with ASR, ST, and NMT tasks simultaneously. Liu et al. (2019) proposed a Knowledge Distillation approach which utilizes a text-only MT model to guide the ST model because there is a huge performance gap between end-to-end ST and MT model. Despite their success, these approaches still need additional labeled data, such as the source language speech, source language transcript, and target language translation.

In this paper, we proposed a new adversarial training method to leverage target monolingual data to relieve the low-resource shortcoming of end-to-end speech translation. The proposed method consists of a generator model and a discriminator model. Specifically, the existing speech translation model is considered as a Generator to gain a target language output, and another neural Discriminator is used to guide the distinction between outputs of speech translation model and true target monolingual sentences. In particular, the Generator and the Discriminator

Proceedings of the 1st Workshop on Automatic Simultaneous Translation, pages 10–14

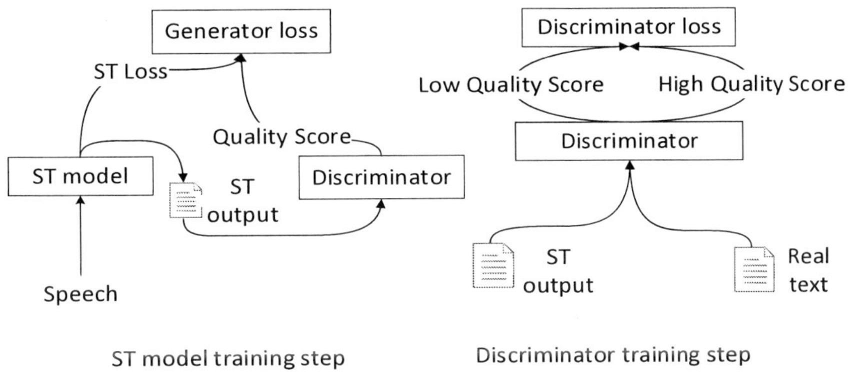

Figure 1: Proposed end-to-end speech translation with adversarial training

are trained iteratively to challenge and learn from each other step by step to gain a better speech translation model. Experimental results on CCMT 2019-BSTC dataset speech translation task demonstrate that the proposed methods can significantly improve the performance of the end-to-end speech translation system.

2 Proposed Method

The framework for the method of adversarial training consists of a generator and a discriminator. In this paper, Generator is the existing end-to-end ST model, which is based on the encoder-decoder model with an attention mechanism (Bérard et al., 2016). The discriminator is a model based on a convolutional neural network, and the output is a quality score. The discriminator is aiming to get higher quality scores for real text and lower quality scores for the output of the ST model in the discriminator training step. In other words, the discriminator is expected to distinguish the input text as much as possible. Meanwhile, our method can not only leverage the ground truth to supervise the training of ST model, but also make use of the discriminator to enhance the output of the ST model by using target monolingual data, as shown in Figure 1.

2.1 Generator

For the end-to-end speech translate, we chose an encoder-decoder model with attention. It takes as an input sequence of audio features $x = (x_1, x_2, \cdots, x_t)$ and a output sequence of words $y = (y_1, y_2, \cdots, y_m)$. The speech encoder is a pyramid bidirectional long short term memory (pBLSTM) (Chan et al., 2016; Hochreiter and Schmidhuber, 1997). It transforms the speech feature $x = (x_1, x_2, \cdots, x_t)$ into a high level representation $H = (h_1, h_2, \cdots, h_n)$, where $n \leq t$. In the pBLSTM, the outputs of two adjacent time steps of the current layer are concatenated and passed to the next layer.

$$h_j^i = \text{pBLSTM}(h_{j-1}^i, [h_{2j}^{i-1}, h_{2j+1}^{i-1}]). \tag{1}$$

Also, the pBLSTM can reduce the length of the encoder input from t to n. In our experiment, we stack 3 layers of the pBLSTM, so we were able to reduce the time step 8 times. The decoder is an attention-based LSTM, and it is a word-level decoder.

$$\begin{aligned} c_i &= \text{Attention}(s_i, h), \\ s_i &= \text{LSTM}(s_{i-1}, c_{i-1}, y_{i-1}), \\ y_i &= \text{Generate}(s_i, c_i), \end{aligned} \tag{2}$$

where the Attention function is a location-aware attention mechanism (Chorowski et al., 2015), and the Generate function is a feed-forward network to compute a score for each symbol in target vocabulary.

2.2 Discriminator

Discriminator takes either real text or ST translations as input and outputs a scalar QS as the quality score. For the discriminator, we use a traditional convolution neural network (CNN) (Kalchbrenner et al., 2016) which focuses on capturing local repeating features and has a better computational efficiency than recurrent neural network (RNN) (LeCun et al., 2015). The real text of the target language is encoded as a sequence of one-hot vectors $y = (y_1, y_2, \cdots, y_m)$, and the output generated by the ST model is denoted as a sequence of vectors $\widetilde{y} = (\widetilde{y}_1, \widetilde{y}_2, \cdots, \widetilde{y}_n)$. The sequence of vectors y or $\widetilde{y}$ are given as input to a single layer neural network. The output of the neural network is fed into a stack of two one-dimensional CNN layers and an average pooling layer. Then we use a linear layer to get the quality score. Training the discriminator is easy to overfit because the probability distribution for ST model output is different from the one-hot encoding of the real text. To address this problem, we used earth-mover distance in WGAN (Martin Arjovsky and Bottou, 2017) to estimate the distance between the ST model output and real text. The loss function of the discriminator is the standard WGAN loss, and adds a gradient penalty(Gulrajani et al., 2017). Formally, the loss function of the discriminator as below:

$$\begin{aligned}\text{Loss}_D = \lambda_1\{\mathbb{E}_{\tilde{y}\sim P_{st}}[D(\tilde{y})] - \mathbb{E}_{y\sim P_{real}}[D(y)]\} \\ + \lambda_2\mathbb{E}_{\hat{y}\sim P_{\hat{y}}}[(\nabla_{\hat{y}}||D(\hat{y})|| - 1)^2],\end{aligned} \quad (3)$$

where λ_1 and λ_2 are hyper-parameter, P_{st} is the distribution of ST model $\tilde{y}$ and P_{real} is the distribution of real text y, $D(y)$ is the quality score for y given by discriminator, $\hat{y}$ are samples generate by randomly interpolating between $\tilde{y}$ and y.

2.3 Adversarial Training

Both the ST model and the discriminator are trained iteratively from scratch. For the ST model training step, the parameters of discriminator are fixed. We train the ST model by minimizing the sequence loss Loss_{ST} which is the cross-entropy between the ground truth and output of the ST model. And at the same time, the discriminator generates a quality score QS for the output of the ST model. Formally, the final loss function in the training process is as follows,

$$\text{Loss}_G = \lambda_{st}\text{Loss}_{ST} - (1 - \lambda_{st})QS, \quad (4)$$

where $\lambda_{st} \in$ [0,1] is hyper-parameter. For the discriminator training step, the parameters of ST model are fixed. The discriminator uses the probability distribution of the ST model output and the real text for training. The specific learning process is shown in Algorithm 1. Note that the discriminator is only used in the training of the model while it is not used during the decoding. Once the training ends, the ST model implicitly utilizes the translation knowledge learned from discriminator to decode the input audio.

Algorithm 1 Adversarial Training

Require: G, the Generator; D, the Discriminator; dataset(X,Y), speech translation parallel corpus.

Ensure: G', generator after adversarial training.

```
for iteration of adversarial training do
    for iteration of training G do
        Sample a subset(X_batch,Y_batch) from dataset(X,Y)
        Y'_batch=G(batch)
        Use Eq.4 as loss function and compute the loss
        Update parameters of G with optimization algorithm
    end for
    for iteration of training Discriminator D do
        Sample a subset(X_batch,Y_batch) from dataset(X,Y)
        Y'_batch=G(batch)
        Let Y_batch as y , Y'_batch as ỹ, use Eq.3 as loss function and compute the loss
        Update parameters of D with optimization algorithm
    end for
end for
```

3 Experiment

3.1 Data Set

We conduct experiments on CCMT 2019-BSTC (Yang et al., 2019) which is collected from the Chinese mandarin talks and reports as shown in Table 1. It contains 50 hours of real speeches, including three parts, the audio files in Chinese, the transcripts, and the English translations. We keep the original data partitions of the data set and segmented the long conversations used for simultaneous interpretation into short utterances.

Dataset	Utterances	Hours
Train	28239	41.4
Valid	956	1.3
Test	569	1.5

Table 1: Size of the CCMT 2019-BSTC.

3.2 Experimental Settings

We process Speech files, to extract 40-dimensional Filter bank features with a step size of 10ms and window size of 25ms. To shorten the training time, we ignored the utterances in the corpus that were longer than 30 seconds. We lowercase and tokenize all English text, and normalize the punctuation. a word-level vocabulary of size 17k is used for target language in English. Then the text data are represented by sequences of 1700-dimensional one-hot vectors. Our ST model uses 3 layers of pBLSTM with 256 units per direction as the encoder, and 512-dimensional location-aware attention was used in the attention layer. The decoder was a 2 layers LSTM with 512 units and 2 layers neural network with 512 units to predict words in the vocabulary. For the discriminator model, we use a linear layer with 128 units at the bottom of the model. Then, using 2 layers one-dimensional CNN, from bottom to top, the window size is 2, the stride is 1, and the window size is 3, the stride is 1. Adam (Kingma and Ba, 2014) was used as the optimization function to train our model, which has a learning rate of 0.0001 and a mini-batch size of 8. The hyper-parameters λ_{st}, λ_1 and λ_2 are 0.5, 0.0001 and 10 respectively. And the train frequency of the ST model is 5 times then the discriminator.

We used the BLEU (Papineni et al., 2002) metric to evaluate our ST models. We try five settings on Speech Translation. The Pipeline model cascades an ASR and an MT model. For the ASR model, we use an end-to-end speech recognition model similar to LAS and trained on CCMT 2019-BSTC. For the MT model, we use open source toolkit OpenNMT (Klein et al., 2017) to train an NMT model. The end-to-end model (described in section 2) does not make any use of source language transcripts. The pre-trained model is the same as the end-to-end model, but its encoder is initialized with a pre-trained ASR model. And the pre-trained ASR model is trained using Aishell (Bu et al., 2017), a 178 hours Chinese Mandarin speech corpus, which has the same language as our chosen speech translation corpus. The multitask model is a one-to-many method, where the ASR and ST tasks share an encoder. The Adversarial Training is the approach proposed in this paper.

3.3 Results

Table 2 shows the result of the different models on the validation set of CCMT 2019-BSTC. From this result, we can find that the end-to-end methods including pre-trained, multitask and Adversarial Training all get results comparable to the Pipeline model. Among them, the pre-trained model gets the best results. Our analysis is that this model uses a larger scale of speech corpus for pre-training, thus introducing more information into the model. We can see that the Adversarial Training method can obtain 19.1 BLEU, which is an improvement of 1.4 BLEU over the end-to-end baseline model, and even better than the multitask method. The multitasking approach uses transcription of source language speech, and our proposed approach is superior to it without using other information.

Model	ST
pipeline	19.4
end-to-end	17.7
pre-trained	20.4
multitask	18.9
Adversarial Training	19.1

Table 2: BLEU scores of the speech translation experiments

4 Conclusion

In this paper, we present the Adversarial Training approach to improve the end-to-end speech translation model. We applied GAN to the speech translation task and achieved good results in the experimental results. Since GAN's structure is used, this method can be applied to any end-to-end speech translation model. Unlike the multitask, pre-trained, and knowledge distillation previously proposed, this method requires the use of additional parallel corpus, which is very expensive to collect. In the future, we will experiment with unpaired text in order to be able to use this method to utilize an infinite amount of spoken text.

References

Antonios Anastasopoulos and David Chiang. 2018. Tied multitask learning for neural speech translation. *arXiv preprint arXiv:1802.06655*.

Dzmitry Bahdanau, Kyunghyun Cho, and Yoshua Bengio. 2014. Neural machine translation by jointly learning to align and translate. *arXiv preprint arXiv:1409.0473*.

Sameer Bansal, Herman Kamper, Karen Livescu, Adam Lopez, and Sharon Goldwater. 2018. Pre-training on high-resource speech recognition improves low-resource speech-to-text translation. *arXiv preprint arXiv:1809.01431*.

Alexandre Bérard, Laurent Besacier, Ali Can Kocabiyikoglu, and Olivier Pietquin. 2018. End-to-end automatic speech translation of audiobooks. In *2018 IEEE International Conference on Acoustics, Speech and Signal Processing (ICASSP)*, pages 6224–6228. IEEE.

Alexandre Bérard, Olivier Pietquin, Christophe Servan, and Laurent Besacier. 2016. Listen and translate: A proof of concept for end-to-end speech-to-text translation. *arXiv preprint arXiv:1612.01744*.

Hui Bu, Jiayu Du, Xingyu Na, Bengu Wu, and Hao Zheng. 2017. Aishell-1: An open-source mandarin speech corpus and a speech recognition baseline. In *2017 20th Conference of the Oriental Chapter of the International Coordinating Committee on Speech Databases and Speech I/O Systems and Assessment (O-COCOSDA)*, pages 1–5. IEEE.

W. Chan, N. Jaitly, Q. Le, and O. Vinyals. 2016. Listen, attend and spell: A neural network for large vocabulary conversational speech recognition. In *2016 IEEE International Conference on Acoustics, Speech and Signal Processing (ICASSP)*, pages 4960–4964.

C. Chiu, T. N. Sainath, Y. Wu, R. Prabhavalkar, P. Nguyen, Z. Chen, A. Kannan, R. J. Weiss, K. Rao, E. Gonina, N. Jaitly, B. Li, J. Chorowski, and M. Bacchiani. 2018. State-of-the-art speech recognition with sequence-to-sequence models. In *2018 IEEE International Conference on Acoustics, Speech and Signal Processing (ICASSP)*, pages 4774–4778.

Jan K Chorowski, Dzmitry Bahdanau, Dmitriy Serdyuk, Kyunghyun Cho, and Yoshua Bengio. 2015. Attention-based models for speech recognition. In *Advances in neural information processing systems*, pages 577–585.

Long Duong, Antonios Anastasopoulos, David Chiang, Steven Bird, and Trevor Cohn. 2016. An attentional model for speech translation without transcription. In *Proceedings of the 2016 Conference of the North American Chapter of the Association for Computational Linguistics: Human Language Technologies*, pages 949–959.

Ishaan Gulrajani, Faruk Ahmed, Martin Arjovsky, Vincent Dumoulin, and Aaron C Courville. 2017. Improved training of wasserstein gans. In *Advances in neural information processing systems*, pages 5767–5777.

Sepp Hochreiter and Jürgen Schmidhuber. 1997. Long short-term memory. *Neural computation*, 9(8):1735–1780.

Nal Kalchbrenner, Lasse Espeholt, Karen Simonyan, Aaron van den Oord, Alex Graves, and Koray Kavukcuoglu. 2016. Neural machine translation in linear time. *arXiv preprint arXiv:1610.10099*.

Diederik P Kingma and Jimmy Ba. 2014. Adam: A method for stochastic optimization. *arXiv preprint arXiv:1412.6980*.

Guillaume Klein, Yoon Kim, Yuntian Deng, Jean Senellart, and Alexander M Rush. 2017. Opennmt: Open-source toolkit for neural machine translation. *arXiv preprint arXiv:1701.02810*.

Yann LeCun, Yoshua Bengio, and Geoffrey Hinton. 2015. Deep learning. *nature*, 521(7553):436–444.

Yuchen Liu, Hao Xiong, Zhongjun He, Jiajun Zhang, Hua Wu, Haifeng Wang, and Chengqing Zong. 2019. End-to-end speech translation with knowledge distillation. *arXiv preprint arXiv:1904.08075*.

SC Martin Arjovsky and Leon Bottou. 2017. Wasserstein generative adversarial networks. In *Proceedings of the 34 th International Conference on Machine Learning, Sydney, Australia*.

Kishore Papineni, Salim Roukos, Todd Ward, and Wei-Jing Zhu. 2002. Bleu: a method for automatic evaluation of machine translation. In *Proceedings of the 40th annual meeting on association for computational linguistics*, pages 311–318. Association for Computational Linguistics.

Ron J Weiss, Jan Chorowski, Navdeep Jaitly, Yonghui Wu, and Zhifeng Chen. 2017. Sequence-to-sequence models can directly translate foreign speech. *arXiv preprint arXiv:1703.08581*.

Muyun Yang, Xixin Hu, Hao Xiong, Jiayi Wang, Yiliyaer Jiaermuhamaiti, Zhongjun He, Weihua Luo, and Shujian Huang. 2019. Ccmt 2019 machine translation evaluation report. In *China Conference on Machine Translation*, pages 105–128. Springer.

Robust Neural Machine Translation with ASR Errors

Haiyang Xue[†], **Yang Feng**[†], **Shuhao Gu**[†], **Wei Chen**[‡]
[†] Key Laboratory of Intelligent Information Processing
Institute of Computing Technology, Chinese Academy of Sciences
[‡] AI Interaction Division, Sogou Inc., Beijing
xuehaiyang,fengyang,gushuhao19b@ict.ac.cn
chenweibj8871@sogou-inc.com

Abstract

In many practical applications, neural machine translation systems have to deal with the input from automatic speech recognition (ASR) systems which may contain a certain number of errors. This leads to two problems which degrade translation performance. One is the discrepancy between the training and testing data and the other is the translation error caused by the input errors may ruin the whole translation. In this paper, we propose a method to handle the two problems so as to generate robust translation to ASR errors. First, we simulate ASR errors in the training data so that the data distribution in the training and test is consistent. Second, we focus on ASR errors on homophone words and words with similar pronunciation and make use of their pronunciation information to help the translation model to recover from the input errors. Experiments on two Chinese-English data sets show that our method is more robust to input errors and can outperform the strong Transformer baseline significantly.

1 Introduction

In recent years, neural machine translation (NMT) has achieved impressive progress and has shown superiority over statistical machine translation (SMT) systems on multiple language pairs (Sennrich et al., 2016). NMT models are usually built under the encoder-decoder architecture where the encoder produces a representation for the source sentence and the decoder generates target translation from this representation word by word (Cho et al., 2014; Sutskever et al., 2014; Gehring et al., 2017; Vaswani et al., 2017). Now NMT systems are widely used in real world and in many cases they receive as input the result of the automatic speech recognition (ASR) system.

Despite the great success, NMT is subject to orthographic and morphological errors which can be comprehended by human (Belinkov and Bisk, 2017). Due to the auto-regression of decoding process, translation errors will be accumulated along with the generated sequence. Once a translation error occurs at the beginning, it will lead to a totally different translation. Although ASR technique is mature enough for commercial applications, there are still recognition errors in their output. These errors from ASR systems will bring about translation errors even totally meaning drift. As the increasing of ASR errors, the translation performance will decline gradually (Le et al., 2017). Moreover, the training data used for NMT training is mainly human-edited sentence pairs in high quality and thus ASR errors in the input are always unseen in the training data. This discrepancy between training and test data will further degrade the translation performance. In this paper, we propose a robust method to address the above two problems introduced by ASR input. Our method not only tries to keep the consistency of the training and test data but to correct the input errors introduced by ASR systems.

We focus on the most widely existent substitution errors in ASR results which can be further distinguished into wrong substitution between words with similar pronunciation and wrong substitution between the words with the same pronunciation (known as homophone words). Table 1 shows Chinese-to-English translation examples of these two kinds of errors. Although only one input word changes in the given three source sentences, their translations are quite different. To keep the consistency between training and testing, we simulate these two types of errors and inject them into the training data randomly. To recover from ASR errors, we integrate the pronunciation information into the translation model to recover the two kinds of errors. For words with similar pronunciation(we name it as Sim-Pron-Words), we first predict the

Proceedings of the 1st Workshop on Automatic Simultaneous Translation, pages 15–23
July 10, 2020.

Gold input	这	份	礼	物	饱	含	一	份	深	情.
	zhè	fèn	lǐ	wù	bǎo	hán	yī	fèn	**shēn**	**qíng**.
ASR-HM	这	份	礼	物	饱	含	一	份	申	请.
	zhè	fèn	lǐ	wù	bǎo	hán	yī	fèn	shēn	qǐng.
ASR-SP	这	份	礼	物	饱	含	一	份	心	情.
	zhè	fèn	lǐ	wù	bǎo	hán	yī	fèn	xīn	qíng.
Reference	This gift is full of affection.									
Trans-HM	This gift contains an application.									
Trans-SP	This gift is full of mood.									

Table 1: A Chinese-English translation example with ASR errors. "ASR-HM" gives an input sentence with ASR errors on homophone words and "Trans-HM" shows its translation. "ASR-SP" gives an input sentence with ASR errors on words with similar pronunciation and "Trans-SP" denotes its translation.

true pronunciation and then integrate the predicted pronunciation into the translation model. For homophone words, although the input characters are wrong, the pronunciation is correct and can be used to assistant translation. In this way, we get a two-stepped method for ASR inputted translation. The first step is to get a training data close to the practical input, so that they can have similar distribution. The second step is to smooth ASR errors according to the pronunciation.

We conducted experiments on two Chinese-to-English data sets and added noise to the test data sets at different rates. The results show that our method can achieve significant improvements over the strong Transformer baseline and is more robust to input errors.

2 Background

As our method is based on the self-attention based neural machine translation model (Transformer) (Vaswani et al., 2017), we will first introduce Transformer briefly before introducing our method.

2.1 Encoder and Decoder

Encoder The encoder consists of 6 identical layers. Each layer consists of two sub-layers: self-attention followed by a position-wise fully connected feed-forward layer. It uses residual connections around each of the sub-layers, followed by layer normalization. The output of each sub-layer is $\mathrm{LayerNorm}(x + \mathrm{Sublayer}(x))$, where $\mathrm{Sublayer}(x)$ is the function carried out by the sub-layer itself. The input sequence $\mathbf{x}$ is fed into these two sub-layers, then we can get the hidden state sequence of the encoder:

$$\mathbf{h} = (\mathbf{h}_1, \mathbf{h}_2, \ldots, \mathbf{h}_j)$$

where j denotes the length of the input sentence.

Decoder The decoder shares a similar structure with the encoder, which also consists of 6 layers. Each layer has three sub-layers: self-attention, encoder-decoder attention and a position-wise feed-forward layer. It also employs a residual connection and layer normalization at each sub-layer. The decoder uses masking in its self-attention to prevent a given output position from incorporating information about future output positions during training.

2.2 Attention

The attention mechanism in Transformer is the so-called scaled dot product attention which uses the dot-product of the query and keys to present the relevance of the attention distribution:

$$\mathbf{a} = softmax(\frac{\mathbf{QK}^T}{\sqrt{d_k}}) \tag{1}$$

where the d_k is the dimensions of the keys. Then the weighted values are summed together to get the final results:

$$\mathbf{t} = \sum(\mathbf{a} \odot \mathbf{V}) \tag{2}$$

Instead of performing a single attention function with a single version of queries, keys and values, multi-head attention mechanism get h different versions of queries, keys and values with different projection functions:

$$\mathbf{Q}^i, \mathbf{K}^i, \mathbf{V}^i = \mathbf{QW}_i^Q, \mathbf{KW}_i^K, \mathbf{VW}_i^V, i \in [1, h] \tag{3}$$

where $\mathbf{Q}^i, \mathbf{K}^i, \mathbf{V}^i$ are the query , key and value representations of the i-th head respectively. $\mathbf{W}_i^Q, \mathbf{W}_i^K, \mathbf{W}_i^V$ are the transformation matrices. h is the number of attention heads. h attention

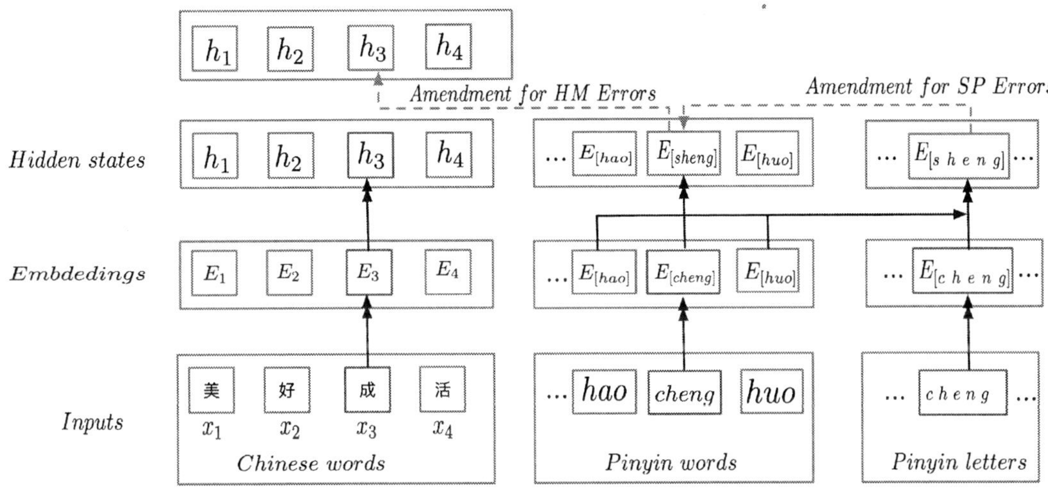

Figure 1: The illustration of our method. "HM" stands for substitution errors between homophone words and "SP" stands for substitution errors between the words with similar pronunciation. The elements in blue boxes are a case of SP errors. Those in the red boxes represent the corrected version with the help of pronunciation information.

Error type	Rate	
Ground Truth	-	语 音 翻 译. yǔ yīn fān yì.
Substitution	6.4%	语 音 翻 一. yǔ yīn fān yī.
Deletion	2.3%	音 翻 译. yīn fān yì.
Insertion	0.7%	语 音 翻 了. yǔ yīn fān le .

Table 2: Word error rate (WER) against all the words for the three types of ASR errors.

functions are applied in parallel to produce the output states $\mathbf{u}_i$. Finally, the outputs are concatenated to produce the final attention:

$$\mathbf{t} = \mathrm{Concat}(\mathbf{t}_1, ..., \mathbf{t}_h) \tag{4}$$

3 The Proposed Method

Although ASR is mature for commercial applications, there are still recognition errors in the result of ASR. The ASR recognition errors can be classified into three categories: *substitution*, *deletion* and *insertion*, which are shown in Table 2. We counted the word error rate (WER) for the three types of errors respectively on our in-house data set, which consists of 100 hours of Chinese speech across multiple domains. The results in Table 2 gives the ratio of the wrong words against the total words. We can see that the substitution errors are the main errors which is consistent with the results in Mirzaei et al. 2016. Other researchers have proven that over 50% of the machine translation errors are associated with substitution errors which have a greater impact on translation quality than deletion or insertion errors (Vilar et al., 2006; Ruiz and Federico, 2014). Substitution errors can be further divided into two categories: substitution between the words with similar pronunciation (denoted as *SP errors*) and substitution between homophone words (denoted as *HM errors*). Based on these conclusions, we focus on these two kinds of substitution errors in this paper. In what follows we will take Chinese as an example to introduce our method and our method can also be applied to many other languages in a similar way.

Our method aims to improve the robustness of NMT to ASR errors. To this end, our method first constructs a training data set which has a similar data distribution with the test data, then makes use of pronunciation information to recover from the SP errors and HM errors. Specifically, our method works in a flow of three steps as

1. adding SP errors and HM errors in the training data randomly to simulate ASR errors occurring in test;
2. predicting the true pronunciation for SP errors and amending the pronunciation to the predicted results;
3. integrating pronunciation information into the

word semantic to assistant the translation of HM errors as homophone words always have the pronunciation.

Figure 1 illustrate the architecture of our method.

Note that the above three steps must be cascaded which means we always first try to correct the pronunciation information for SP errors and then use the corrected pronunciation information to play a part in the translation for HM errors. We will introduce the three steps in details in the following sections.

3.1 Simulating ASR errors in Training

We process source words one by one by first deciding whether to change it to ASR noise at a certain probability $p \in [0, 1]$, and if yes, then selecting one word to substitute the source word according to the word frequency of the training data. Given a source word x, we first collect its SP word set $\mathcal{V}_{sp}(x)$ and HM word set $\mathcal{V}_{hm}(x)$, then sample from a Bernoulli distribution with a probability p to substitute it with a noise:

$$r_x \sim \text{Bernoulli}(p) \tag{5}$$

where $r_x \in \{0, 1\}$ is the output of the Bernoulli distribution and $p \in [0, 1]$ is the probability that the Bernoulli distribution outputs 1. When r_x is 1, we go to the next step to substitute x. Next, we can select a word to substitute x from a word set $\mathcal{V}(x)$ at a probability as

$$p(x) = \frac{\text{Count}(x)}{\sum\limits_{x' \in \mathcal{V}(x) \backslash \{x\}} \text{Count}(x')} \tag{6}$$

where $\text{Count}(x)$ stands for the count that the word x occurs in the training data, and $\mathcal{V}(x)$ can be $\mathcal{V}_{sp}(x)$, $\mathcal{V}_{hm}(x)$ or $\mathcal{V}_{sp}(x) \cup \mathcal{V}_{hm}(x)$ depending on whether we want to simulate SP errors, HM errors or mixture. To get the training data with the data distribution consistent with the ASR input, we sample words from $\mathcal{V}_{sp}(x) \cup \mathcal{V}_{hm}(x)$.

3.2 Amending Pronunciation for SP Errors

In Chinese, the Pinyin word is used to represent the pronunciation of the word and a Pinyin word usually consists of several Pinyin letters. For example, in Table 2, the Pinyin word for the word "语" is "yǔ" and it has two Pinyin letters as "y" and "ǔ". According to the pronunciation, one Pinyin word can be divided into two parts: *the initial*, which usually only contains the first Pinyin letter, and *the final*, which usually contains the rest Pinyin letters. We looked into our in-house ASR results and found that most SP errors are caused by the wrong initial. Besides, Chinese Pinyin has fixed combinations of the initial and the final, and hence given a final, we can get all possible initials that can occur together with the final in one Pinyin word. In this sense, for an SP error, we can draw the distribution over all the possible initials to predict the correct Pinyin word. With the distribution, we can amend the embedding of the Pinyin word to the correct one.

Formally, given a source sentence $\mathbf{x} = (x_1, \ldots, x_J)$, we use $\mathbf{u} = (u_1, \ldots, u_J)$ to denote its Pinyin word sequence and use u_{jk} to denote the k-th Pinyin letter in the Pinyin word u_j. For a Pinyin word u_j, we represent its initial as

$$u_j^{\text{ini}} = u_{j1} \tag{7}$$

and represent its final as

$$u_j^{\text{fin}} = [u_{j2}, \ldots, u_{jK_j}] \tag{8}$$

where K_j is the number of Pinyin letters of u_j. We also maintain an embedding matrix for the Pinyin words and the Pinyin letters, respectively. Then we can get the embedding for the final u_j^{fin} by adding all the embedding of its Pinyin letters as

$$\mathbf{E}[u_j^{\text{fin}}] = \sum_{k=2}^{K_j} (\mathbf{E}[u_{jk}]) \tag{9}$$

where $\mathbf{E}[\cdot]$ means the corresponding embedding of the input. As SP errors usually result from wrong initials, we predict the probability of the true initial according to the co-occurrence with the immediately previous Pinyin word u_{j-1} and the right after Pinyin word u_{j+1}. Then we can draw the distribution over all the possible initials for u_j as

$$p^{\text{ini}} \sim \text{softmax}(g^{\text{ini}}(\mathbf{E}[u_{j-1}] + \mathbf{E}[u_j^{\text{fin}}] + \mathbf{E}[u_{j+1}])) \tag{10}$$

where $g^{\text{ini}}(\cdot)$ is a linear transformation function. Then we use the weighted sum of the embedding of all the possible initials as the true embedding of u_j^{ini} as

$$\mathbf{E}[u_j^{\text{ini}}] = \sum_{l \in \mathcal{V}^{\text{ini}}(u_j)} p^{\text{ini}}(l) * \mathbf{E}[l] \tag{11}$$

where $\mathcal{V}^{\text{ini}}(u_j)$ denotes the letter set which can be used as the initial of u_j and $p^{\text{ini}}(l)$ denotes the predicted probability for the Pinyin letter l in Equation 10. Then we can update the embedding of u_j based on the amended Pinyin letter embedding as

$$\mathbf{E}[u_j] = g(\mathbf{E}[u_j], \mathbf{E}[u_j^{\text{ini}}], \mathbf{E}[u_j^{\text{fin}}]) \quad (12)$$

where $g(.)$ is a linear transformation function.

3.3 Amending Encoding for HM Errors

For HM errors, although the source word is not correct, the Pinyin word is still correct. Therefore, the Pinyin word can be used to provide additional true information about the source word. Specifically, we integrate the embedding of Pinyin words into the final output of the encoder, denoted as $\mathbf{h} = (\mathbf{h}_1, \ldots, \mathbf{h}_J)$, to get an advanced encoding for each source word. This is implemented via a gating mechanism and we calculate the gate λ_j for the j-th source word as

$$\lambda_j = \mathbf{W}_\lambda \tanh(\mathbf{W}_h \mathbf{h}_j + \mathbf{W}_u \mathbf{E}[u_j]) \quad (13)$$

where $\mathbf{W}_\lambda$, $\mathbf{W}_h$ and $\mathbf{W}_u$ are weight matrices. With the gate, we update the hidden state $\mathbf{h}_j$ to

$$\mathbf{h}_j = \lambda_j * \mathbf{h}_j + (1 - \lambda_j) * \mathbf{E}[u_j] \quad (14)$$

Then the updated hidden states of source words are fed to the decoder for the calculation of attention and generation of target words.

4 Experiments

4.1 Data Preparation

We evaluated our method on two Chinese-English data sets which are from the NIST translation task and WMT17 translation task, respectively. For the NIST translation task, the training data consists of about 1.25M sentence pairs from LDC corpora with 27.9M Chinese words and 34.5M English words respectively [1]. We used NIST 02 data set as the development set and NIST 03, 04, 05, 06, 08 sets as the **clean** test sets which don't have ASR errors in the source side. For the WMT17 translation task, the training data consists of 9.3M bilingual sentence pairs obtained by combing the CWMT corpora and News Commentary v12. We use the newsdev2017 and newstest2017 as our development set and clean test set, respectively.

For both of these two corpus, we tokenized and truecased the English sentences using the Moses scripts[2]. Then 30K merging operations were performed to learn byte-pair encoding(BPE) (Sennrich et al., 2015). As for the Chinese data, we split the sentence into Chinese chars. We use the ChineseTone[3] tool to convert Chinese characters into their Pinyin counterpart without tones.

Then we apply the method mentioned in the section 3.1 to add SP errors, HM errors or both to the clean training set to get three kinds of noisy data. We have also set the substituting probability p to 0.1, 0.2 and 0.3 to investigate the impacts of the ASR errors in the training set. Considering that there is no public test sets simulating the substitution errors of ASR, we also crafted another three **noisy** test sets based on the clean sets with different amount of HM errors and SP errors in each source side sentence to test the robustness of the NMT model. We try our best to make these noisy test sets be close to the results of ASR, so that it can check the ability of our proposed method in the realistic speech translation scenario.

4.2 Training Details

We evaluate the proposed method on the Transformer model and implement on the top of an open-source toolkit Fairseq-py (Edunov et al., 2017). We follow (Vaswani et al., 2017) to set the configurations and have reproduced their reported results on the Base model. All the models were trained on a single server with eight NVIDIA TITAN Xp GPUs where each was allocated with a batch size of 4096 tokens. Sentences longer than 100 tokens were removed from the training data. For the base model, we trained it for a total of 100k steps and save a checkpoint at every 1k step intervals. The single model obtained by averaging the last 5 checkpoints were used for measuring the results.

During decoding, we set beam size to 5, and length penalty α=0.6 (Wu et al., 2016). Other training parameters are the same as the default configuration of the Transformer model. We report case-sensitive NIST BLEU (Papineni et al., 2002) scores for all the systems. For evaluation, we first merge output tokens back to their untokenized representation using *detokenizer.pl* and then use *multi-bleu.pl* to compute the scores as per reference.

4.3 Main Results

The main results are shown in the Table 3 and Table 5 (Row1 and Row4). It shows that our propoed

[1]The corpora include LDC2002E18, LDC2003E07, LDC2003E14, Hansards portion of LDC2004T07, LDC2004T08 and LDC2005T06.

[2]http://www.statmt.org/moses/

[3]https://github.com/letiantian/ChineseTone

System	p	Clean	Noise			
			1 Sub	2 Subs	3 Subs	Ave.
Baseline	-	45.21	43.63	42.24	41.33	42.40
Our Method	0.1	45.15	44.64	44.23	43.87	44.24
	0.2	45.13	44.83	44.41	44.12	44.45
	0.3	44.95	44.68	44.45	44.09	44.40

Table 3: Case-sensitive BLEU scores of our approaches on thec NIST clean test set (average bleu score on nist03, nist04, nist05, nist06) and three artificial noisy test sets (1 Sub, 2 Subs and 3 Subs) which are crafted by randomly substituting one, two and three original characters of each source sentence in the clean test set with HM errors or SP errors, respectively. p is the substitution rate.

System	p	Clean	Noise Ave.
Baseline	-	45.21	42.40
+SP Amendment	0.2	45.20	43.55
+HM Amendment	0.2	45.30	43.77
+Both Amendment	0.2	45.13	44.45

Table 4: Results of the ablation study on the NIST data. "+SP Amendment", "+HM Amendmen" and "+Both Amendment" represents the model only with the amending pronunciation for SP errors, amending errors for HM errors and with amending pronunciation for both of these two kinds of errors, respectively.

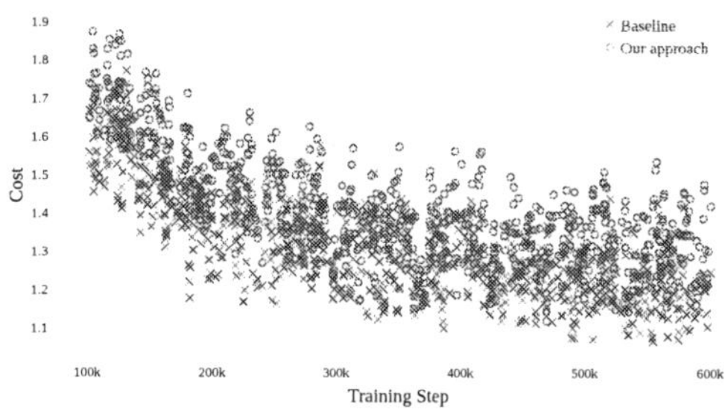

Figure 2: Training cost of the baseline model (blue dots) and our proposed method (red dots).

System	p	Clean	Noise
Baseline	-	23.11	20.23
+SP Amendment	0.2	23.08	22.12
+HM Amendment	0.2	23.09	22.23
+Both Amendment	0.2	23.13	22.67

Table 5: Comparison of "+SP Amendment", "+HM Amendmen" and "+Both Amendment" on the WMT17 ZH→EN dataset.

model significantly outperforms the baseline model on the **noisy** test sets on both of the NIST and WMT17 translation tasks. Furthermore, we got the following conclusions:

First, the baseline model performs well on the **clean** test set, but it suffers a great performance drop on the **noisy** test sets, which indicates that the conventional NMT is indeed fragile to permuted inputs, which is consistent with prior work (Belinkov and Bisk, 2017; Cheng et al., 2018).

Second, the results of our proposed method show that our model can not only get a competitive performance compared to the baseline model on the clean test set, but also outperform all the baseline models on the noisy tests. Moreover, our proposed method doesn't drop so much on the noisy test sets as the ASR errors increase, which proves that our proposed method is more robust to the noisy inputs after we make use of the pronunciation features to amend the representation of the input tokens for the SP errors and HM errors.

Last, we find that our method works best when the hyper-parameter p was set to 0.2 in our experiments. It indicates that the different noise sampling methods have different impacts on the final results. Too few or too much ASR errors simulated in the training data both can't make the model achieve the best performance in practice. This finding can guide us to better simulate the noisy data, thus helping us train a more robust model in the future work.

4.4 Ablation Study

In order to further understand the impact of the components of the proposed method, we performed some further studies by training multiple versions of our model by removing the some components of it. The first one is just with the amending pronunciation for SP errors. The second one is just with the amending errors for HM error. The overall results are shown in the Table 4 and Table 5.

The "+SP Amendment" method also improve the robustness and fault tolerance of the model. It is obvious that in all the cases, our proposed Sim-Pron-Words model outperforms baseline system by +1.15 and + 1.89 BLEU. which indicates that it can also greatly enhance the anti-noise capability of the NMT model.

The "+HM Amendmen" method provides further robustness improvements compared to the baseline system on all the noisy test sets. The results show that the model with SP amendment achieves a further improvement by an average of +1.37 and +2.00 BLEU on the NIST and WMT17 noisy test sets respectively. In addition, it has also achieved a performance equivalent to baseline on the clean test sets. It demonstrates that homophones feature is an effective input feature for improving the robustness of Chinese-sourced NMT.

Eventually, as expectecd, the best performance is obtained with the simultaneous use of all the tested elements, proving that these two features can cooperate with each other to improve the performance further.

4.5 Training Cost

We also investigate the training cost of our proposed method and the baseline system. The loss curves are shown in the Figure 2. It shows that the training cost of our model is higher than the baseline system, which indicates that our proposed model may take more words into consideration when predicting the next word, because it aggregate the pronunciation information of the source side character. Thus we can get a higher BLEU score on the test sets than the baseline system, which will ignore some more appropriate word candidates just without the pronunciation information. The training loss curves and the BLEU results on the test sets show that our approach effectively improves the generalization performance of the conventional NMT model trained on the clean training data.

4.6 Effect of Source Sentence Length

We also evaluate the performance of our proposed method and the baseline on the noisy test sets with different source sentence lengths. As shown in Figure 3, the translation quality of both systems is improved as the length increases and then degrades as the length exceeds 50. Our observation is also consistent with prior work (Bahdanau et al., 2014).

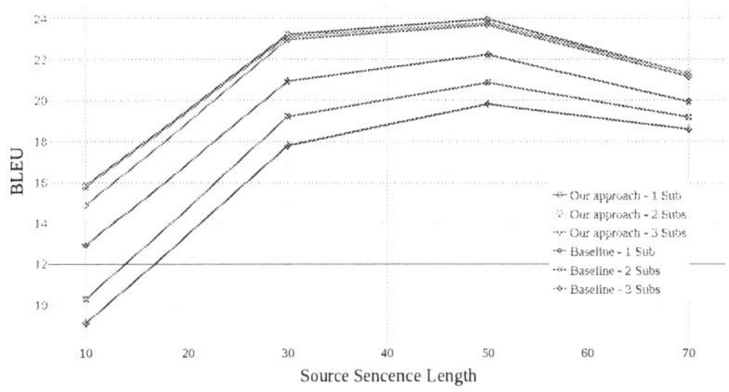

Figure 3: Effect of source sentence lengths of noisy input.

These curves imply that more context is helpful to noise disambiguation. It also can be seen that our robust system outperforms the baseline model on all the noisy test sets in each length interval. Besides, the increasing number of the error in the source sentence doesn't degrade the performance of our proposed model too much, indicating the effectiveness of our method.

4.7 A Case Study

In Table 6, we provide a realistic example to illustrate the advantage of our robust NMT system on erroneous ASR output. For this case, the syntactic structure and meaning of the original sentence are destroyed since the original character "数" which means digit is misrecognized as the character "书" which means book. "数" and "书" share the same pronunciation without tones. Human beings generally have no obstacle to understanding this flawed sentence with the aid of its correct pronunciation. The baseline NMT system can hardly avoid the translation of "书" which is a high-frequency character with explicit word sense. In contrast, our robust NMT system can translate this sentence correctly. We also observe that our system works well even if the original character "数" is substituted with other homophones, such as "舒" which means comfortable. It shows that our system has a powerful ability to recover the minor ASR error. We consider that the robustness improvement is mainly attributed to our proposed ASR-specific noise training and Chinese Pinyin feature.

5 Related Work

It is necessary to enhance the robustness of machine translation since the ASR system carries misrecognized transcriptions over into the downstream MT system in the SLT scenario. Prior work at-

Speech	该 gāi	数 **shù**	字 zì	已 yǐ	经 jīng	大 dà	幅 fú	下 xià	降 jiàng	近 jìn	一 yī	半。 bàn。
ASR	该 gāi	书 **shū**	字 zì	已 yǐ	经 jīng	大 dà	幅 fú	下 xià	降 jiàng	近 jìn	一 yī	半。 bàn。
Ref	The figure has fallen sharply by almost half.											
Baseline	The book has fallen by nearly half.											
Our Approach	The figure has fallen by nearly half.											

Table 6: For the same erroneous ASR output, translations of the baseline NMT system and our robust NMT system.

tempted to induce noise by considering the realistic ASR outputs as the source corpora used for training MT systems (Peitz et al., 2012; Tsvetkov et al., 2014). Although the problem of error propagation could be alleviated by the promising end-to-end speech translation models (Serdyuk et al., 2018; Bérard et al., 2018). Unfortunately, there are few training data in the form of speech paired with text translations. In contrast, our approach utilizes the large-scale written parallel corpora. Recently, Sperber et al. (2017) adapted the NMT model to noise outputs from ASR, where they introduced artificially corrupted inputs during the training process and only achieved minor improvements on noisy input but harmed the translation quality on clean text. However, our approach not only significantly enhances the robustness of NMT on noisy test sets, but also improves the generalization performance.

In the context of NMT, a similar approach was very recently proposed by Cheng et al. (2018), where they proposed two methods of constructing adversarial samples with minor perturbations to train NMT models more robust by supervising both the encoder and decoder to represent similarly for both the perturbed input sentence and its original counterpart. In contrast, our approach has several advantages: 1) our method of constructing noise examples is efficient yet straightforward without expensive computation of words similarity at training time; 2) our method has only one hyper-parameter without putting too much effort into performance tuning; 3) the training of our approach performs efficiently without pre-training of NMT models and complicated discriminator; 4) our approach achieves a stable performance on noise input with different amount of errors.

Our approach is motivated by the work of NMT incorporated with linguistic input features (Sennrich and Haddow, 2016). Chinese linguistic features, such as radicals and Pinyin, have been demonstrated effective to Chinese-sourced NMT (Liu et al., 2019; Zhang and Matsumoto, 2017; Du and Way, 2017) and Chinese ASR (Chan and Lane, 2016). We also incorporate Pinyin as an additional input feature in the robust NMT model, aiming at improving the robustness of NMT further.

6 Conclusion

Voice input has become popular recently and as a result, machine translation systems have to deal with the input from the results of ASR systems which contains recognition errors. In this paper we aim to improve the robustness of NMT when its input contains ASR errors from two aspects. One is from the perspective of data by adding simulated ASR errors to the training data so that the training data and the test data have a consistent distribution. The other is from the perspective of the model itself. Our method takes measures to handle two types of the most widely existent ASR errors: substitution errors between the words with similar pronunciation (SP errors) and substitution errors between homophone words (HM errors). For SP errors, we make use of the context pronunciation information to correct the embedding of Pinyin words. For HM errors, we use pronunciation information directly to amend the encoding of source words. Experiment results prove the effectiveness of our method and the ablation study indicates that our method can handle both the types of errors well. Experiments also show that our method is stable during training and more robust to the errors.

References

Dzmitry Bahdanau, Kyunghyun Cho, and Yoshua Bengio. 2014. Neural machine translation by jointly learning to align and translate. *arXiv preprint arXiv:1409.0473*.

Yonatan Belinkov and Yonatan Bisk. 2017. Synthetic and natural noise both break neural machine translation. In *Proc. ICLR*.

Alexandre Bérard, Laurent Besacier, Ali Can Kocabiyikoglu, and Olivier Pietquin. 2018. End-to-end automatic speech translation of audiobooks. In *Proc. ICASSP*.

William Chan and Ian Lane. 2016. On online attention-based speech recognition and joint mandarin character-pinyin training. In *Proc. Interspeech*.

Yong Cheng, Zhaopeng Tu, Fandong Meng, Junjie Zhai, and Yang Liu. 2018. Towards robust neural machine translation. In *Proc. ACL*, pages 1756–1766.

Kyunghyun Cho, Bart Van Merriënboer, Caglar Gulcehre, Dzmitry Bahdanau, Fethi Bougares, Holger Schwenk, and Yoshua Bengio. 2014. Learning phrase representations using rnn encoder-decoder for statistical machine translation. *arXiv preprint arXiv:1406.1078*.

Jinhua Du and Andy Way. 2017. Pinyin as subword unit for chinese-sourced neural machine translation. In *Irish Conference on Artificial Intelligence and Cognitive Science*.

Sergey Edunov, Myle Ott, and Sam Gross. 2017. https://github.com/pytorch/ fairseq.

Jonas Gehring, Michael Auli, David Grangier, Denis Yarats, and Yann N Dauphin. 2017. Convolutional sequence to sequence learning. *arXiv preprint arXiv:1705.03122*.

Ngoc-Tien Le, Benjamin Lecouteux, and Laurent Besacier. 2017. Disentangling asr and mt errors in speech translation. *arXiv preprint arXiv:1709.00678*.

Hairong Liu, Mingbo Ma, Liang Huang, Hao Xiong, and Zhongjun He. 2019. Robust neural machine translation with joint textual and phonetic embedding. In *Proceedings of the 57th Annual Meeting of the Association for Computational Linguistics*, pages 3044–3049.

Maryam Sadat Mirzaei, Kourosh Meshgi, and Tatsuya Kawahara. 2016. Automatic speech recognition errors as a predictor of l2 listening difficulties. In *Proc. the Workshop on Computational Linguistics for Linguistic Complexity (CL4LC)*, pages 192–201.

Kishore Papineni, Salim Roukos, Todd Ward, and Wei-Jing Zhu. 2002. Bleu: a method for automatic evaluation of machine translation. In *Proc. the 40th annual meeting on association for computational linguistics*, pages 311–318.

Stephan Peitz, Simon Wiesler, Markus Nußbaum-Thom, and Hermann Ney. 2012. Spoken language translation using automatically transcribed text in training. In *Proc. IWSLT*.

Nicholas Ruiz and Marcello Federico. 2014. Assessing the impact of speech recognition errors on machine translation quality. *Association for Machine Translation in the Americas (AMTA), Vancouver, Canada*, pages 261–274.

Rico Sennrich and Barry Haddow. 2016. Linguistic input features improve neural machine translation. In *Proc. WMT*.

Rico Sennrich, Barry Haddow, and Alexandra Birch. 2015. Neural machine translation of rare words with subword units. *arXiv preprint arXiv:1508.07909*.

Rico Sennrich, Barry Haddow, and Alexandra Birch. 2016. Edinburgh neural machine translation systems for wmt 16. In *Proc. the First Conference on Machine Translation*.

Dmitriy Serdyuk, Yongqiang Wang, Christian Fuegen, Anuj Kumar, Baiyang Liu, and Yoshua Bengio. 2018. Towards end-to-end spoken language understanding. *arXiv preprint arXiv:1802.08395*.

Matthias Sperber, Graham Neubig, Jan Niehues, and Alex Waibel. 2017. Neural lattice-to-sequence models for uncertain inputs. *arXiv preprint arXiv:1704.00559*.

Ilya Sutskever, Oriol Vinyals, and Quoc V Le. 2014. Sequence to sequence learning with neural networks. In *Advances in neural information processing systems*, pages 3104–3112.

Yulia Tsvetkov, Florian Metze, and Chris Dyer. 2014. Augmenting translation models with simulated acoustic confusions for improved spoken language translation. Proc. ACL.

Ashish Vaswani, Noam Shazeer, Niki Parmar, Jakob Uszkoreit, Llion Jones, Aidan N Gomez, Łukasz Kaiser, and Illia Polosukhin. 2017. Attention is all you need. In *Advances in Neural Information Processing Systems*, pages 6000–6010.

David Vilar, Jia Xu, D'Haro Luis Fernando, and Hermann Ney. 2006. Error analysis of statistical machine translation output. In *Proc. LREC*, pages 697–702.

Yonghui Wu, Mike Schuster, Zhifeng Chen, Quoc V Le, Mohammad Norouzi, Wolfgang Macherey, Maxim Krikun, Yuan Cao, Qin Gao, Klaus Macherey, et al. 2016. Google's neural machine translation system: Bridging the gap between human and machine translation. *arXiv preprint arXiv:1609.08144*.

Jinyi Zhang and Tadahiro Matsumoto. 2017. Improving character-level japanese-chinese neural machine translation with radicals as an additional input feature. In *Asian Language Processing (IALP), 2017 International Conference on*, pages 172–175. IEEE.

Improving Autoregressive NMT with Non-Autoregressive Model

Long Zhou[1,2], Jiajun Zhang[1,2], Chengqing Zong[1,2,3]
[1]National Laboratory of Pattern Recognition, CASIA, Beijing, China
[2]School of Artificial Intelligence, University of Chinese Academy of Sciences, Beijing, China
[3]CAS Center for Excellence in Brain Science and Intelligence Technology, Shanghai, China
{long.zhou, jjzhang, cqzong}@nlpr.ia.ac.cn

Abstract

Autoregressive neural machine translation (NMT) models are often used to teach non-autoregressive models via knowledge distillation. However, there are few studies on improving the quality of autoregressive translation (AT) using non-autoregressive translation (NAT). In this work, we propose a novel ***Encoder-NAD-AD*** framework for NMT, aiming at boosting AT with global information produced by NAT model. Specifically, under the semantic guidance of source-side context captured by the encoder, the non-autoregressive decoder (NAD) first learns to generate target-side hidden state sequence in parallel. Then the autoregressive decoder (AD) performs translation from left to right, conditioned on source-side and target-side hidden states. Since AD has global information generated by low-latency NAD, it is more likely to produce a better translation with less time delay. Experiments on WMT14 En⇒De, WMT16 En⇒Ro, and IWSLT14 De⇒En translation tasks demonstrate that our framework achieves significant improvements with only 8% speed degeneration over the autoregressive NMT.

1 Introduction

Neural machine translation (NMT) based on *encoder-decoder* framework has gained rapid progress over recent years (Sutskever et al., 2014; Bahdanau et al., 2015; Wu et al., 2016; Gehring et al., 2017; Vaswani et al., 2017; Zhang and Zong, 2020). All these high-performance NMT models generate target languages from left to right in an autoregressive manner. An obvious limitation of autoregressive translation (AT) is that the inference process can hardly be parallelized, and the inference time is linear with respect to the length of the target sequence.

To speed up the inference of machine translation,

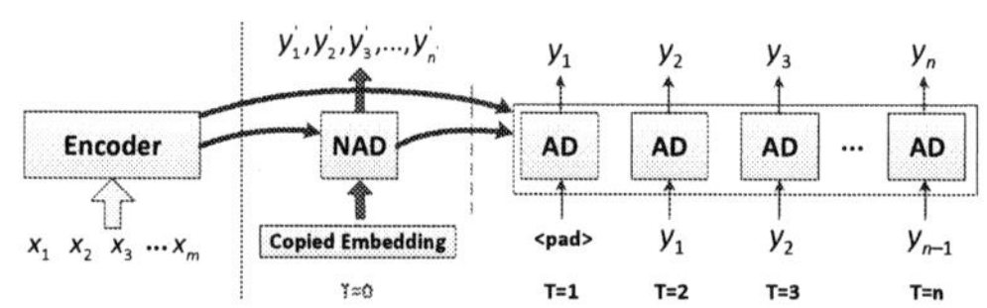

Figure 1: Decoding illustration of our proposed *Encoder-NAD-AD* framework including an encoder, non-autoregressive decoder (NAD) and autoregressive decoder (AD).

non-autoregressive translation (NAT) models have been proposed, which generate all target tokens independently and simultaneously (Gu et al., 2017; Lee et al., 2018; Kaiser et al., 2018; Libovický and Helcl, 2018). Although NAT is successfully trained with the help from an AT model as its teacher via knowledge distillation (Kim and Rush, 2016), there is no work focusing on improving the quality of AT using NAT. Therefore, a natural question arises, *can we boost AT with NAT?*

In this paper, we propose a novel and effective *Encoder-NAD-AD* framework for NMT, in which the newly added non-autoregressive decoder (NAD) can provide target-side global information when autoregressive decoder (AD) translates, as illustrated in Figure 1. Briefly speaking, the encoder is first used to encode the source sequence into a sequence of vector representations. NAD then reads the encoder representations and generates a coarse target sequence in parallel. Given the source-side and target-side contexts separately captured by the encoder and NAD, AD learns to generate final translation token by token.

Our proposed model can fully combine two major advantages compared to previous work (Vaswani et al., 2017; Xia et al., 2017). On the one hand, due to the lower latency during inference of NAT, the decoding efficiency of our proposed framework is only slightly lower than

Proceedings of the 1st Workshop on Automatic Simultaneous Translation, pages 24–29

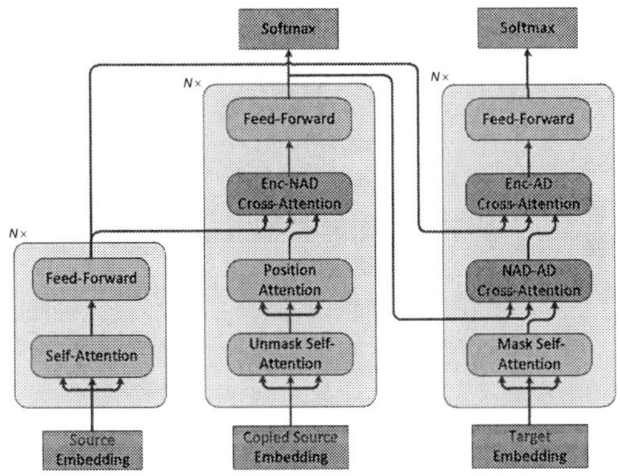

Figure 2: The extended Transformer translation model that exploits global information produced by NAT. We omit the residual connection and layer normalization in each sub-layer for simplicity.

the standard NMT models, as shown in Figure 1. On the other hand, since AD can asses the global target-side context provided by NAD, it has the potential to generate a better translation by fully exploiting source-side and target-side contexts. We conduct massive experiments on WMT14 En⇒De, WMT16 En⇒Ro and IWSLT14 De⇒En translations tasks. Experimental results demonstrate that our proposed model achieves substantial improvements with only 8% degradation in decoding efficiency compared to the standard NMT.

2 The Framework

Our goal in this work is to improve autoregressive NMT using the non-autoregressive model with lower latency during inference. Figure 2 shows the model architecture of the proposed framework. Next, we will detail individual components and introduce an algorithm for training and inference.

2.1 The Neural Encoder

The neural encoder of our model is identical to that of the dominant Transformer model, which is modeled using the self-attention network. The encoder is composed of a stack of N identical layers, each of which has two sub-layers:

$$\begin{aligned} \widetilde{h}^l &= \text{LN}(h^{l-1} + \text{MHAtt}(h^{l-1}, h^{l-1}, h^{l-1})) \\ h^l &= \text{LN}(\widetilde{h}^l + \text{FFN}(\widetilde{h}^l)) \end{aligned} \tag{1}$$

where the superscript l indicates layer depth, h^l denotes the source hidden state of l-th layer, LN is layer normalization, FFN means feed-forward networks, and MHAtt denotes the multi-head attention mechanism (Vaswani et al., 2017).

2.2 Non-Autoregressive Decoder

We initialize the non-autoregressive decoder inputs using copied source inputs from the encoder side by the fertility mechanism (Gu et al., 2017). For each layer in non-autoregressive decoder, the lowest sub-layer is the unmasked multi-head self-attention network, and it also uses residual connections around each of the sublayers, followed by layer normalization.

$$z_1^l = \text{LN}(z^{l-1} + \text{MHAtt}(z^{l-1}, z^{l-1}, z^{l-1})) \tag{2}$$

The second sub-layer is a positional attention. We follow (Gu et al., 2017) and use the positional encoding p as both query and key and the decoder states as the value:

$$z_2^l = \text{LN}(z_1^l + \text{MHAtt}(z_1^l, p^l, p^l)) \tag{3}$$

The third sub-layer is Enc-NAD cross-attention that integrates the representation of corresponding source sentence, and the fourth sub-layer is a FFN:

$$\begin{aligned} z_3^l &= \text{LN}(z_2^l + \text{MHAtt}(z_2^l, h^N, h^N)) \\ z^l &= \text{LN}(z_3^l + \text{FFN}(z_3^l)) \end{aligned} \tag{4}$$

where h^N is the source hidden state of top layer.

2.3 Autoregressive Decoder

For each layer in autoregressive decoder, the lowest sub-layer is the masked multi-head self-attention network:

$$s_1^l = \text{LN}(s^{l-1} + \text{MHAtt}(s^{l-1}, s^{l-1}, s^{l-1})) \tag{5}$$

The second sub-layer is NAD-AD cross-attention that integrates non-autoregressive sequence context into autoregressive decoder:

$$s_2^l = \text{LN}(s_1^l + \text{MHAtt}(s_1^l, z^N, z^N)) \tag{6}$$

In addition, the decoder both stacks Enc-AD cross-attention and FFN sub-layers to seek task-relevant input semantics to bridge the gap between the input and output languages:

$$\begin{aligned} s_3^l &= \text{LN}(s_2^l + \text{MHAtt}(s_2^l, h^N, h^N)) \\ s^l &= \text{LN}(s_3^l + \text{FFN}(s_3^l)) \end{aligned} \tag{7}$$

2.4 Training and Inference

Given a set of training examples $\{x^{(z)}, y^{(z)}\}_{z=1}^Z$, the training algorithm aims to find the model parameters that maximize the likelihood of the training

#	System	Architecture	En⇒De	En⇒Ro	De⇒En
		Existing NAT Systems			
1	(Gu et al., 2017)	NAT	17.35	26.22	-
2	(Lee et al., 2018)	NAT-IR (adaptive)	18.91	-	-
3	(Wang et al., 2019)	NAT-AR	20.61	-	23.89
		Existing AT Systems			
4	(Wu et al., 2016)	Google-NMT	24.60	-	-
5	(Gehring et al., 2017)	ConvS2S	26.36	-	-
6	(Vaswani et al., 2017)	Transformer	27.30	-	-
7	(Xia et al., 2017)	Deliberate Network	27.56	33.18	33.95
		Our NMT Systems			
8		Transformer	27.06	32.28	32.87
9	*this work*	NAT	21.25	26.60	27.06
10		Our Model	**27.65**†	**33.17**⇑	**34.01**⇑

Table 1: Comparing with existing NMT systems on WMT14 En⇒De, WMT16 En⇒Ro, and IWSLT14 De⇒En test sets. "†/⇑" indicates statistically significant (p<0.05/0.01) from the Transformer baseline.

data:

$$J(\theta) = \frac{1}{Z}\sum_{z=1}^{Z}\{log\ P(y_{ad}^{(z)}|x^{(z)}, \theta_{enc}, \theta_{nad}, \theta_{ad}) \\ +\lambda * log\ P(\widetilde{y}_{nad}^{(z)}|x^{(z)}, \theta_{enc}, \theta_{nad})\} \quad (8)$$

where $\widetilde{y}_{nad}$ is the reference of NAT, which can be obtained from standard NMT model via sequence-level knowledge distillation (Gu et al., 2017; Lee et al., 2018; Wang et al., 2019), and λ is a hyperparameter used to balance the preference between the two terms. Once our model is trained, we use the decoding algorithm shown in Figure 1 to translate source language with little time wasted over the autoregressive NMT.

3 Experiments

We use 4-gram NIST BLEU (Papineni et al., 2002) as the evaluation metric, and *sign-test* (Collins et al., 2005) to test for statistical significance.

3.1 Datasets

We conduct experiments on three widely used public machine translation corpora: WMT14 English-German[2] (En⇒De), WMT16 English-Romanian[3] (En⇒Ro), and IWSLT14 German-English[4] (De⇒En), whose training sets consist of 4.5M, 600K, 153K sentence pairs, respectively. We employ 37K, 40K, and 10K shared BPE (Sennrich et al., 2016) tokens for En⇒De, En⇒Ro, and De⇒en respectively. For En⇒De, we use `newstest2013` as the validation set and `newstest2014` as the test set. For En⇒Ro, we use `newsdev-2016` and `newstest-2016` as development and test sets. For De⇒En, we use 7K data split from the training set as the validation set and use the concatenation of `dev2010`, `tst2010`, `tst2011`, and `tst2012` as the test set, which is widely used in prior works (Bahdanau et al., 2017; Wang et al., 2019).

3.2 Model Settings

We build the described models modified from the open-sourced tensor2tensor[5] toolkit. For our proposed model, we employ the Adam optimizer with β_1=0.9, β_2=0.998, and ϵ=10^{-9}. For En⇒De and En⇒Ro, we use the hyperparameter settings of `base` Transformer model as Vaswani et al. (2017), whose encoder and decoder both have 6 layers, 8 attention-heads, and 512 hidden sizes. We follow Gu et al. (2017) to use the same `small` Transformer setting for IWSLT14 because of its smaller dataset. For evaluation, we use argmax decoding for NAD, and beam search with a beam size of k=4 and length penalty α=0.6 for AD. We also re-implement and compare with deliberate network (Xia et al., 2017) based on strong Transformer, which adopts the two-pass decoding method and uses the autoregressive decoding manner for the first decoder.

[2] http://www.statmt.org/wmt14/translation-task.html
[3] http://www.statmt.org/wmt16/translation-task.html.
[4] https://wit3.fbk.eu/
[5] https://github.com/tensorflow/tensor2tensor

Models	Latency	Degeneration
Transformer	251ms	0%
Deliberate Network	422ms	68%
NAT	16ms	(16× speedup)
Our Model	271ms	8%

Table 2: Decoding efficiency of different models. Latency is computed as average of per sentence decoding time on the test set of De⇒En.

3.3 Results and Analysis

In this section, we evaluate and analyze the proposed approach on En⇒De, En⇒Ro, and De⇒En translation tasks.

Model Complexity We first compare the model parameters and training speed in De⇒En for Transformer baseline, deliberate network, and our proposed model, which have 10.3M, 16.3M, and 18.0M parameters, respectively. Although our model uses more parameter than deliberate network due to additional position attention network, its training speed is significantly faster than deliberate network (1.8 steps/s vs. 0.7 steps/s)

Translation Quality We report the translation performance in Table 1, from which we can make the following conclusions: (1) Our proposed model (row 10) significantly outperforms Transformer baseline (row 8) by 0.59, 0.89, and 1.14 BLEU points in three translation tasks, respectively. (2) Compared to the existing deliberate network which uses greedy search for the one-pass decoding, our model can obtain a comparable performance. (3) Our NAT model (row 9) can achieve a competitive or even better model accuracy than previous NAT models (rows 1-3).

Decoding Speed Table 2 shows the decoding efficiency of different models. The deliberate network achieves the translation improvement at the cost of the substantial drop in decoding speed (68% degeneration). However, due to the high efficiency during inference of non-autoregressive models (16× speedup than Transformer), the decoding efficiency of our proposed framework is only slightly lower (8% degeneration) than the standard autoregressive Transformer models.

Case Study To better understand how our model works, we present a translation example sampled form De⇒En task in Table 3. The standard AT model incorrectly translates the phrase "geschrieben sein könnte" into "may be", and omits word "geschrieben". This problem is well addressed by the *Encoder-NAD-AD* framework, since AD can access the global information contained in the draft sequence generated by NAD, and therefore outputs a better sentence.

Source	ich sage dann mit meinen eigenen worten, was zwischen diesem gerüst geschrieben sein könnte .
Reference	then i will say , in my own words , what could be written within this framework .
AT	i then say to my own words , which *may be* between that framework .
NAT	i i say with my own words , which could be written between this scaffold .
Our Model	i then say , in my own words , what could be written between this framework ?

Table 3: Translation examples from De⇒En task. The *italic fonts* indicate the incomplete translation problem.

4 Related Work

There are many design choices in the *encoder-decoder* framework based on different types of layers, such as RNN-based (Sutskever et al., 2014), CNN-based (Gehring et al., 2017), and self-attention based (Vaswani et al., 2017) approaches. Particularly, relying entirely on the attention mechanism, the Transformer introduced by Vaswani et al. (2017) can improve the training speed as well as model performance.

In term of speeding up the decoding of the neural Transformer, Gu et al. (2017) modified the autoregressive architecture to directly generate target words in parallel. In past two years, non-autoregressive and semi-autoregressive models have been extensively studied (Oord et al., 2017; Kaiser et al., 2018; Lee et al., 2018; Libovický and Helcl, 2018; Wang et al., 2019; Guo et al., 2018; Zhou et al., 2019a). Previous work shows that NAT can be improved via knowledge distillation from AT models. In contrast, the idea of improving AT with NAT is not well explored.

The most relevant to our proposed framework is deliberation network (Xia et al., 2017), which leverages the global information by observing both back and forward information in sequence decoding through a deliberation process. Recently, Zhang et al. (2018) proposed asynchronous bidirectional decoding for NMT (ABD-NMT), which extended the conventional encoder-decoder framework by introducing a backward decoder. Different from ABD-NMT, synchronous bidirectional sequence generation model perform left-to-right decoding and right-to-left decoding simultaneously and interactively (Zhou et al., 2019b; Zhang et al., 2020). Besides, Geng et al. (2018) introduced a adaptive multi-pass decoder to standard NMT models. However, the above models improve translation quality while greatly reducing inference efficiency.

5 Conclusion

In this work, we propose a novel *Encoder-NAD-AD* framework for NMT, aiming at improving the quality of autoregressive decoder with global information produced by the newly added non-autoregressive decoder. We extensively evaluate the proposed model on three machine translation tasks (En⇒De, En⇒Ro, and De⇒En). Compared to existing deliberation network (Xia et al., 2017) which suffers from serious decoding speed degradation, our proposed model achieves a significant improvement in translation quality with little degradation of decoding efficiency compared to the state-of-the-art autoregressive NMT.

References

Dzmitry Bahdanau, Philemon Brakel, Kelvin Xu, Anirudh Goyal, Ryan Lowe, Joelle Pineau, Aaron Courville, and Yoshua Bengio. 2017. An actor-critic algorithm for sequence prediction. *In Proceedings of ICLR 2017*.

Dzmitry Bahdanau, Kyunghyun Cho, and Yoshua Bengio. 2015. Neural machine translation by jointly learning to align and translate. *In Proceedings of ICLR 2015*.

Michael Collins, Philipp Koehn, and Ivona Kučerová. 2005. Clause restructuring for statistical machine translation. In *Proceedings of the 43rd annual meeting on association for computational linguistics*, pages 531–540. Association for Computational Linguistics.

Jonas Gehring, Michael Auli, David Grangier, Denis Yarats, and Yann N. Dauphin. 2017. Convolutional sequence to sequence learning. In *Proceedings of the 34th International Conference on Machine Learning*, volume 70 of *Proceedings of Machine Learning Research*, pages 1243–1252, International Convention Centre, Sydney, Australia. PMLR.

Xinwei Geng, Xiaocheng Feng, Bing Qin, and Ting Liu. 2018. Adaptive multi-pass decoder for neural machine translation. In *Proceedings of the 2018 Conference on Empirical Methods in Natural Language Processing*, pages 523–532, Brussels, Belgium. Association for Computational Linguistics.

Jiatao Gu, James Bradbury, Caiming Xiong, Victor OK Li, and Richard Socher. 2017. Non-autoregressive neural machine translation. In *Proceedings of ICLR 2017*.

Junliang Guo, Xu Tan, Di He, Tao Qin, Linli Xu, and Tie-Yan Liu. 2018. Non-autoregressive neural machine translation with enhanced decoder input. In *Proceedings of AAAI 2019*.

Łukasz Kaiser, Aurko Roy, Ashish Vaswani, Niki Pamar, Samy Bengio, Jakob Uszkoreit, and Noam Shazeer. 2018. Fast decoding in sequence models using discrete latent variables. In *Proceedings of ICML 2018*.

Yoon Kim and Alexander M. Rush. 2016. Sequence-level knowledge distillation. In *Proceedings of the 2016 Conference on Empirical Methods in Natural Language Processing*, pages 1317–1327. Association for Computational Linguistics.

Jason Lee, Elman Mansimov, and Kyunghyun Cho. 2018. Deterministic non-autoregressive neural sequence modeling by iterative refinement. In *Proceedings of the 2018 Conference on Empirical Methods in Natural Language Processing*, pages 1173–1182, Brussels, Belgium. Association for Computational Linguistics.

Jindřich Libovický and Jindřich Helcl. 2018. End-to-end non-autoregressive neural machine translation with connectionist temporal classification. In *Proceedings of the 2018 Conference on Empirical Methods in Natural Language Processing*, pages 3016–3021, Brussels, Belgium. Association for Computational Linguistics.

Aaron van den Oord, Yazhe Li, Igor Babuschkin, Karen Simonyan, Oriol Vinyals, Koray Kavukcuoglu, George van den Driessche, Edward Lockhart, Luis C Cobo, Florian Stimberg, et al. 2017. Parallel wavenet: Fast high-fidelity speech synthesis. *arXiv preprint arXiv:1711.10433*.

Kishore Papineni, Salim Roukos, Todd Ward, and Wei-Jing Zhu. 2002. Bleu: a method for automatic evaluation of machine translation. In *Proceedings of the 40th annual meeting on association for computational linguistics*, pages 311–318. Association for Computational Linguistics.

Rico Sennrich, Barry Haddow, and Alexandra Birch. 2016. Neural machine translation of rare words with subword units. In *Proceedings of the 54th Annual Meeting of the Association for Computational Linguistics (Volume 1: Long Papers)*, pages 1715–1725. Association for Computational Linguistics.

Ilya Sutskever, Oriol Vinyals, and Quoc V Le. 2014. Sequence to sequence learning with neural networks. In Z. Ghahramani, M. Welling, C. Cortes, N. D. Lawrence, and K. Q. Weinberger, editors, *Advances in Neural Information Processing Systems 27*, pages 3104–3112. Curran Associates, Inc.

Ashish Vaswani, Noam Shazeer, Niki Parmar, Jakob Uszkoreit, Llion Jones, Aidan N Gomez, Ł ukasz Kaiser, and Illia Polosukhin. 2017. Attention is all you need. In I. Guyon, U. V. Luxburg, S. Bengio, H. Wallach, R. Fergus, S. Vishwanathan, and R. Garnett, editors, *Advances in Neural Information Processing Systems 30*, pages 5998–6008. Curran Associates, Inc.

Yiren Wang, Fei Tian, Di He, Tao Qin, ChengXiang Zhai, and Tie-Yan Liu. 2019. Non-autoregressive machine translation with auxiliary regularization. In *Proceedings of AAAI 2019*.

Yonghui Wu, Mike Schuster, Zhifeng Chen, Quoc V Le, Mohammad Norouzi, Wolfgang Macherey, Maxim Krikun, Yuan Cao, Qin Gao, Klaus Macherey, Jeff Klingner, Apurva Shah, Melvin Johnson, Xiaobing Liu, Lukasz Kaiser, Stephan Gouws, Yoshikiyo Kato, Taku Kudo, Hideto Kazawa, Keith Stevens, George Kurian, Nishant Patil, Wei Wang, Cliff Young, Jason Smith, Jason Riesa, Alex Rudnick, Oriol Vinyals, Greg Corrado, Macduff Hughes, and Jeffrey Dean. 2016. Google's neural machine translation system: Bridging the gap between human and machine translation. *arXiv preprint arXiv:1609.08144*.

Yingce Xia, Fei Tian, Lijun Wu, Jianxin Lin, Tao Qin, Nenghai Yu, and Tie-Yan Liu. 2017. Deliberation networks: Sequence generation beyond one-pass decoding. In I. Guyon, U. V. Luxburg, S. Bengio, H. Wallach, R. Fergus, S. Vishwanathan, and R. Garnett, editors, *Advances in Neural Information Processing Systems 30*, pages 1784–1794. Curran Associates, Inc.

Jiajun Zhang, Long Zhou, Yang Zhao, and Chengqing Zong. 2020. Synchronous bidirectional inference for neural sequence generation. *Artif. Intell.*, 281:103234.

Jiajun Zhang and Chengqing Zong. 2020. Neural machine translation: Challenges, progress and future. volume abs/2004.05809.

Xiangwen Zhang, Jinsong Su, Yue Qin, Yang Liu, Rongrong Ji, and Hongji Wang. 2018. Asynchronous bidirectional decoding for neural machine translation. *In Proceedings of AAAI 2018*.

Long Zhou, Jiajun Zhang, Heng Yu, and Chengqing Zong. 2019a. Sequence generation: From both sides to the middle. In *Proceedings of IJCAI 2019*.

Long Zhou, Jiajun Zhang, and Chengqing Zong. 2019b. Synchronous bidirectional neural machine translation. *Transactions of the Association for Computational Linguistics*, 7:91–105.

Modeling Discourse Structure for Document-level Neural Machine Translation

Junxuan Chen[1]*, **Xiang Li**[2], **Jiarui Zhang**[1], **Chulun Zhou**[1], **Jianwei Cui**[2], **Bin Wang**[2], **Jinsong Su**[1]†

[1]Xiamen University, Xiamen, China

[2]Xiaomi AI Lab, Xiaomi Inc., Beijing, China

{chenjx,zhangjiarui,clzhou}@stu.xmu.edu.cn jssu@xmu.edu.cn

{lixiang21,cuijianwei,wangbin11}@xiaomi.com

Abstract

Recently, document-level neural machine translation (NMT) has become a hot topic in the community of machine translation. Despite its success, most of existing studies ignored the discourse structure information of the input document to be translated, which has shown effective in other tasks. In this paper, we propose to improve document-level NMT with the aid of discourse structure information. Our encoder is based on a hierarchical attention network (HAN) (Miculicich et al., 2018). Specifically, we first parse the input document to obtain its discourse structure. Then, we introduce a Transformer-based path encoder to embed the discourse structure information of each word. Finally, we combine the discourse structure information with the word embedding before it is fed into the encoder. Experimental results on the English-to-German dataset show that our model can significantly outperform both Transformer and Transformer+HAN.

1 Introduction

Neural machine translation (NMT) has made great progress in the past decade. In practical applications, the need for NMT systems has expanded from individual sentences to complete documents. Therefore, document-level NMT has gradually drawn much more attention. Contextual information is particularly important for obtaining high-quality document translation. To get better contextual information, researchers have proposed many methods (e.g., memory network and hierarchical attention network) for document-level translation (Sim Smith, 2017; Tiedemann and Scherrer, 2017; Wang et al., 2017a; Tu et al., 2017; Wang et al., 2017a; Voita et al., 2018; Zhang et al., 2018; Miculicich et al., 2018; Maruf and Haffari, 2018; Maruf et al., 2019; Yang et al., 2019). Discourse structure, as well as raw contextual sentences, is a major component of the document. And it has been proved to be effective in many other tasks, such as automatic document summarization (Yoshida et al., 2014; Isonuma et al., 2019) and sentiment classification (Schouten and Frasincar, 2016; Nejat et al., 2017). However, to the best of our knowledge, discourse structure has not been explicitly used in document-level NMT.

To address the above problem, we propose to improve document-level NMT with the aid of discourse structure information. First, we represent each input document with a Rhetorical Structure Theory-based discourse tree (Mann and Thompson, 1988). Then, we use a Transformer-based path encoder to embed the discourse structure path of each word and combine it with the corresponding word embedding before feeding it into the sentence encoder. In this way, discourse structure information can be fully exploited to enrich word representations and guide the context encoder to capture the relevant context of the current sentence. Finally, we adopt HAN (Miculicich et al., 2018) as our context encoder to model context information in a hierarchical manner.

Our contributions are as follows: (i) We propose a novel and efficient approach to explicitly exploit discourse structure information for document-level NMT. Particularly, our approach is applicable for any other context encoder of document-level NMT; (ii) We carry out experiments on English-to-German translation task and experimental results show that our model outperforms competitive baselines.

*This work is done when Junxuan Chen was interning at Xiaomi AI Lab, Xiaomi Inc., Beijing, China.

†Corresponding author.

Proceedings of the 1st Workshop on Automatic Simultaneous Translation, pages 30–36

July 10, 2020.

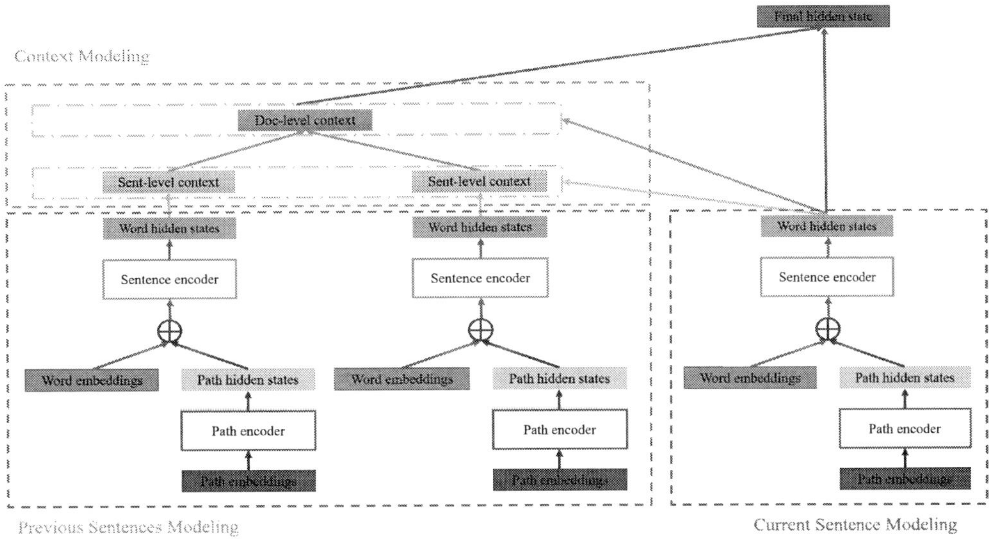

Figure 1: The architecture of our proposed encoder

2 Related Work

In the era of statistical machine translation, document-level machine translation has become one of the research focuses in the community of machine translation. (Xiao et al., 2011; Su et al., 2012; Xiao et al., 2012; Su et al., 2015). Recently, with the rapid development of NMT, document-level NMT has also gradually attracted people's attention (Voita et al., 2018; Maruf and Haffari, 2018; Miculicich et al., 2018; Maruf et al., 2019; Yang et al., 2019). Typically, existing studies aim to improve document-level translation quality with the help of document context, which is usually extracted from neighboring sentences of the current sentence. For example,some researchers applied cache-based models to selectively remember the most relevant context information of the document (Voita et al., 2018; Maruf and Haffari, 2018; Kuang et al., 2018), while some researchers employed hierarchical context networks to catch document context information for Transformer (Miculicich et al., 2018; Maruf et al., 2019; Yang et al., 2019). Specifically, Miculicich et al. (2018) proposed a hierarchical attention network to model contextual information, Maruf et al. (2019) applied a selective attention method to select contextual information that is more relevant to the current sentence, and Yang et al. (2019) employed capsule network to model multi-angle context information.

Although these methods have made some progress in document-level NMT, they all ignored the discourse structure information, which can be used to not only enrich word embedding but also guide the selection of relevant context for the current sentence.

3 Our Encoder

We propose a novel document-level NMT model based on HAN (Miculicich et al., 2018). The difference between ours and HAN lies in that we introduce the RST-based discourse structure to represent the document-level context, which is incorporated into HAN to refine translation.

Figure 1 gives the architecture of our proposed encoder. In addition to the standard encoder for the current sentence, it contains HAN (Miculicich et al., 2018) as context encoder, and a novel path encoder for the discourse structure. We first use the Transformer-based path encoder to model discourse structure information. Then, we combine the embedding of each input word with its corresponding path embedding vector and feed the combined vector into the sentence encoder. Finally, we use the hierarchical attention network to capture the global contextual embedding and update the hidden states of current sentence as the final output of the whole encoder.

In our model, the translation of a document is made by translating each of its sentences sequentially. We introduce discourse structure for both the current sentence and contextual sentences. Given a source document X, the translation probability of

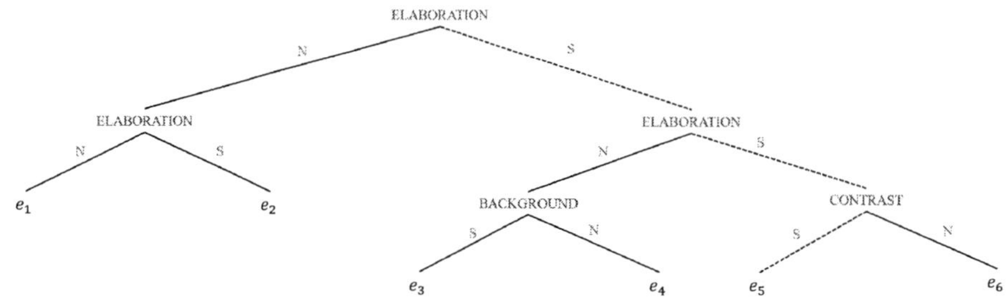

1. [For example, one important achievement of former President Felipe Calderón's administration was to push through a 140-mile highway]e_1 [connecting the interior city of Durango and the Pacific port at Mazatlán.]e_2
2. [Traversing extremely rough terrain with 200 tunnels and bridges,]e_3 [it promises to cut the transit time by three or four hours.]e_4
3. **[Except for the weather,]e_5 [the highway has the feel of Switzerland.]e_6**

Figure 2: An example discourse tree of with six EDUs. N and S denote the relative importance label *NUCLEUS* and *SATELLITE*, respectively. Sentence 3 is the current sentence to be translated, with two previous context sentences 1 and 2. On the tree, the path marked with dotted lines from the root node to the leaf node e_5 is used to represent the discourse structure of e_5.

the target document Y can be defined as:

$$P(Y \mid X; \theta) = \prod_{j=1}^{J} P(Y^j \mid X^j, D^j, S; \theta), \quad (1)$$

where X^j and Y^j denote the j-th source sentence and its target translation respectively, D^j denotes the contextual sentences, S represents the discourse structure of the document to be translated, and θ is the parameter set of the model.

3.1 RST-based Discourse Structure

For each document to be translated, we parse it to obtain its discourse structure based on Rhetorical Structure Theory (RST) (Mann and Thompson, 1988). RST is one of the most influential theories of document coherence. According to RST, we represent each document with a hierarchical tree. As shown in Figure 2, the discourse tree contains some leaf nodes, each of which indicates an Elementary Discourse Unit (EDU). The adjacent leaf nodes are recursively connected into units by certain coherence relations (e.g., *ELABORATION, BACKGROUND*) until the entire tree is built. Besides, *NUCLEUS* or *SATELLITE* is used to mark the relative importance of child node units in the relationship.

In this work, we represent the discourse structure information of each word using its discourse path from root node to its corresponding leaf node. Each path is a mixed label sequence composed of the discourse relationship and the importance label (e.g., *NUCLEUS_ELABORATION, SATELLITE_BACKGROUND*). Please note that all tokens in the same EDU share the same discourse structure. For example, the discourse structure of EDU e_5 is "*SATELLITE_ELABORATION SATELLITE_ELABORATION SATELLITE_CONTRAST*".

3.2 Discourse Structure Path Embedding

To integrate the structural information of words into the our HAN-based document-level NMT model, we first additionaly introduce a Transformer-based path encoder to encode discourse structure paths of words. Specifically, for each word w_i, we directly consider its discourse structure path p_i as a sequence and then employ the path encoder to learn its contextual hidden states, which can be finally averaged to produce the overall discourse embedding vector d_i. Then, we enrich each input word embedding with its corresponding discourse embedding vector before it is fed into the context encoder or the translation encoder. Concretely, for the word w_i, we define its enriched vector as the sum of its word embedding and discourse embedding: $\widetilde{x_i} = x_i + d_i$.

3.3 HAN-based Context Modeling

Following (2018), we apply hierarchical attention network (HAN) as our context encoder. Due to the advantage of accurately capturing different levels of contexts, HAN has been widely used in many tasks, such as document classification (Yang et al., 2016), stance detection (Sun et al., 2018), sentence-level NMT (Su et al., 2018b). Using this encoder, we mainly focus on two levels of context modeling:

Sentence-level Context Modeling For the i-th word of the current sentence, we employ muti-head attention (Vaswani et al., 2017) to summarize the context from the k-th context sentence:

$$cs_{i,k} = \text{MultiHead}(f_s(h_i), \mathbf{H_k}), \quad (2)$$

where f_s is a linear transformation function, h_i denotes the hidden state representation of the i-th token of current sentence. By doing so, our context encoder can exploit different types of relation between words to better capture sentence-level context. And $\mathbf{H_k}$ is the hidden state representation of the k-th context sentence and is used as value and key for attention.

Document-level Context Modeling Unlike the above modeling, here we mainly on capturing the context information from previous K sentences for the i-th word of the current sentence.

$$cd_i = \text{FFN}(\text{MultiHead}(f_d(h_i), \mathbf{CS_i})), \quad (3)$$

where f_d is a linear transformation, and $\mathbf{CS_i} = [cs_{i,1}, cs_{i,2}, \cdots, cs_{i,K}]$ is the sentence-level context of K contextual sentences.

Integrating Document-level Context into the Translation Encoder Finally, we integrate the above-mentioned document-level context into the translation encoder via a gating operation:

$$\lambda_i = \sigma(\mathbf{W_h} h_i + \mathbf{W_{cd}} cd_i) \quad (4)$$

$$\widetilde{h_i} = \lambda_i h_i + (1 - \lambda_i) cd_i \quad (5)$$

where $\mathbf{W_h}$ and $\mathbf{W_{cd}}$ denote parameter matrices for h_i and cd_i, and $\widetilde{h_i}$ is the final output of the encoder.

4 Experiments

4.1 Settings

Datasets We conduct our experiments on English-to-German translation task. The sentence-aligned document-delimited News Comment v11 corpus [1], the WMT16 newstest2015 and the newstest2016 are used as the training set, development and test set, respectively.

We download all the above corpus from (Maruf et al., 2019), of which statistics are provided in Table 1.

[1]http://www.casmacat.eu/corpus/news-commentary.html

	#Sentences	Document length
Training	236,287	38.93
Development	2,169	26.78
Test	2,999	19.35

Table 1: The statistical of our datasets. #Sentence indicates the number of sentences, and Document length means the average number of sentences in document.

Settings We use Transformer (Vaswani et al., 2017) as our context-agnostic baseline system and Transformer+HAN (Miculicich et al., 2018) as our context-aware baseline system. We conduct experiments using the same configuration as HAN. Specifically, both sentence encoder and decoder are composed of 6 hidden layers, while path encoder is composed of 2 hidden layers. We use three previous sentences as contextual sentences for current sentence. The hidden size and point-wise FFN size are 512 and 2048 respectively. The dropout rates for all hidden states are set to 0.1. The source and target vocabulary sizes are both 30K. At the training phase, we use the Adam optimizer (Kingma and Ba, 2015) and the batch sizes of context-agnostic model and context-aware model are 4096 and 1024, respectively. Finally, we use case-sensitive BLEU (Papineni et al., 2002) and TER (Snover et al., 2006) to measure the translation quality.

Data Preprocessing All datasets are tokenized and truecased using the scripts of Moses Toolkit (Koehn et al., 2007). We split them into subword units using a joint bye pair encoding model with 30K merge operations. To get discourse structure of the input documents, we first apply the open-source tool NeuralEDUSeg (Wang et al., 2018) obtaining non-overlapping EDUs. Then, we employ StageDP (Wang et al., 2017b) to obtain discourse structure trees of segmented documents. Afterwards, we extract the path from root node to leaf node as the discourse structure information for the corresponding EDU, where all words share the same discourse structure path.

4.2 Results and Analysis

Table 2 shows the experimental results for different models. The sentence-level Transformer, context-agnostic baseline, obtains a result of 22.78 BLEU and 59.3 TER, while the context-aware baseline Transformer+HAN (Miculicich et al., 2018) obtains 24.45 BLEU and 56.9 TER. The sentence-

Model	BLEU	TER
Transformer	22.78	59.3
Transformer+DS	23.61 (+0.83)	58.5 (-0.8)
Transformer+HAN	24.45 (+1.67)	56.9 (-2.4)
Transformer+HAN+DS	**24.84** (+2.06)	**56.4** (-2.9)

Table 2: BLEU and TER scores for different models. The best scores are marked in bold. HAN denotes Hierarchical Attention Network which is used to get context information while DS denotes Discourse Structure information.

level Transformer integrated with discourse structure achieves an improvement of 0.83 on BLEU and a decline of 0.8 on TER. By contrast, our model integrated with contextual information and discourse structure information further gains a better performance, 2.06 higher than Transformer and 0.39 higher than Transformer+HAN on BLEU, 2.9 lower than Transformer and 0.5 lower than Transformer+HAN on TER.

Our experimental results show that discourse structure features indeed provide helpful information to enhance the translation quality of both context-agnostic and context-aware document-level NMT models. Please note that our approach is also applicable to other document-level NMT models.

5 Conclusion

This paper has presented a novel discourse structure-based encoder for document-level NMT. The main idea of our encoder lies in enriching the input word embeddings with their path embeddings based on discourse structure. Experimental results on English-to-German translation verify the effectiveness of our proposed encoder.

In the future, we plan to extend our encoder to other NLP tasks, such as simultaneous translation. Simultaneous translation, as well as document-level NMT, has difficulty in modeling the long context so that it may be effective to improve the re-translation with the structure information modeled by our encoder. Finally, we will focus on refining document-level NMT with variational neural networks, which has shown effecitive in previous studies of sentence-level NMT (Zhang et al., 2016; Su et al., 2018a).

Acknowledgments

This work was supported by the National Key R&D Program of China under Grant 2019QY1803, the National Natural Science Foundation of China (No. 61672440), and the Scientific Research Project of National Language Committee of China (No. YB135-49).

References

Masaru Isonuma, Junichiro Mori, and Ichiro Sakata. 2019. Unsupervised neural single-document summarization of reviews via learning latent discourse structure and its ranking. In *Proceedings of the 57th Annual Meeting of the Association for Computational Linguistics*, pages 2142–2152, Florence, Italy. Association for Computational Linguistics.

Diederik P. Kingma and Jimmy Ba. 2015. Adam: A method for stochastic optimization. *CoRR*, abs/1412.6980.

Philipp Koehn, Hieu Hoang, Alexandra Birch, Chris Callison-Burch, Marcello Federico, Nicola Bertoldi, Brooke Cowan, Wade Shen, Christine Moran, Richard Zens, Chris Dyer, Ondřej Bojar, Alexandra Constantin, and Evan Herbst. 2007. Moses: Open source toolkit for statistical machine translation. In *Proceedings of the 45th Annual Meeting of the Association for Computational Linguistics Companion Volume Proceedings of the Demo and Poster Sessions*, pages 177–180, Prague, Czech Republic. Association for Computational Linguistics.

Shaohui Kuang, Deyi Xiong, Weihua Luo, and Guodong Zhou. 2018. Modeling coherence for neural machine translation with dynamic and topic caches. In *Proceedings of the 27th International Conference on Computational Linguistics*, pages 596–606, Santa Fe, New Mexico, USA. Association for Computational Linguistics.

William C. Mann and Sandra A. Thompson. 1988. Rhetorical structure theory: Toward a functional theory of text organization. *Text Talk*, 8(3):243–281.

Sameen Maruf and Gholamreza Haffari. 2018. Document context neural machine translation with memory networks. In *Proceedings of the 56th Annual Meeting of the Association for Computational Linguistics (Volume 1: Long Papers)*, pages 1275–1284, Melbourne, Australia. Association for Computational Linguistics.

Sameen Maruf, André F. T. Martins, and Gholamreza Haffari. 2019. Selective attention for context-aware neural machine translation. In *Proceedings of the*

2019 Conference of the North American Chapter of the Association for Computational Linguistics: Human Language Technologies, Volume 1 (Long and Short Papers), pages 3092–3102, Minneapolis, Minnesota. Association for Computational Linguistics.

Lesly Miculicich, Dhananjay Ram, Nikolaos Pappas, and James Henderson. 2018. Document-level neural machine translation with hierarchical attention networks. In *Proceedings of the 2018 Conference on Empirical Methods in Natural Language Processing*, pages 2947–2954, Brussels, Belgium. Association for Computational Linguistics.

Bita Nejat, Giuseppe Carenini, and Raymond Ng. 2017. Exploring joint neural model for sentence level discourse parsing and sentiment analysis. In *Proceedings of the 18th Annual SIGdial Meeting on Discourse and Dialogue*, pages 289–298, Saarbrücken, Germany. Association for Computational Linguistics.

Kishore Papineni, Salim Roukos, Todd Ward, and Wei-Jing Zhu. 2002. Bleu: a method for automatic evaluation of machine translation. In *Proceedings of the 40th Annual Meeting of the Association for Computational Linguistics*, pages 311–318, Philadelphia, Pennsylvania, USA. Association for Computational Linguistics.

Kim Schouten and Flavius Frasincar. 2016. COMMIT at SemEval-2016 task 5: Sentiment analysis with rhetorical structure theory. In *Proceedings of the 10th International Workshop on Semantic Evaluation (SemEval-2016)*, pages 356–360, San Diego, California. Association for Computational Linguistics.

Karin Sim Smith. 2017. On integrating discourse in machine translation. In *Proceedings of the Third Workshop on Discourse in Machine Translation*, pages 110–121, Copenhagen, Denmark. Association for Computational Linguistics.

Matthew Snover, Bonnie Dorr, Richard Schwartz, Linnea Micciulla, and John Makhoul. 2006. A study of translation edit rate with targeted human annotation. In *Proceedings of AMTA 2006*.

Jinsong Su, Hua Wu, Haifeng Wang, Yidong Chen, Xiaodong Shi, Huailin Dong, and Qun Liu. 2012. Translation model adaptation for statistical machine translation with monolingual topic information. In *Proceedings of the 50th Annual Meeting of the Association for Computational Linguistics (Volume 1: Long Papers)*, pages 459–468, Jeju Island, Korea. Association for Computational Linguistics.

Jinsong Su, Shan Wu, Deyi Xiong, Yaojie Lu, Xianpei Han, and Biao Zhang. 2018a. Variational recurrent neural machine translation. In *Thirty-Second AAAI Conference on Artificial Intelligence*.

Jinsong Su, Deyi Xiong, Yang Liu, Xianpei Han, Hongyu Lin, Junfeng Yao, and Min Zhang. 2015. A context-aware topic model for statistical machine translation. In *Proceedings of the 53rd Annual Meeting of the Association for Computational Linguistics and the 7th International Joint Conference on Natural Language Processing (Volume 1: Long Papers)*, pages 229–238, Beijing, China. Association for Computational Linguistics.

Jinsong Su, Jiali Zeng, Deyi Xiong, Yang Liu, Mingxuan Wang, and Jun Xie. 2018b. A hierarchy-to-sequence attentional neural machine translation model. *IEEE/ACM Transactions on Audio, Speech, and Language Processing*, 26(3):623–632.

Qingying Sun, Zhongqing Wang, Qiaoming Zhu, and Guodong Zhou. 2018. Stance detection with hierarchical attention network. In *Proceedings of the 27th International Conference on Computational Linguistics*, pages 2399–2409, Santa Fe, New Mexico, USA. Association for Computational Linguistics.

Jörg Tiedemann and Yves Scherrer. 2017. Neural machine translation with extended context. In *Proceedings of the Third Workshop on Discourse in Machine Translation*, pages 82–92, Copenhagen, Denmark. Association for Computational Linguistics.

Zhaopeng Tu, Yang Liu, Zhengdong Lu, Xiaohua Liu, and Hang Li. 2017. Context gates for neural machine translation. *Transactions of the Association for Computational Linguistics*, 5:87–99.

Ashish Vaswani, Noam Shazeer, Niki Parmar, Jakob Uszkoreit, Llion Jones, Aidan N. Gomez, Lukasz Kaiser, and Illia Polosukhin. 2017. Attention is all you need. *In Advances in neural information processing systems*, pages 5998—-6008.

Elena Voita, Pavel Serdyukov, Rico Sennrich, and Ivan Titov. 2018. Context-aware neural machine translation learns anaphora resolution. In *Proceedings of the 56th Annual Meeting of the Association for Computational Linguistics (Volume 1: Long Papers)*, pages 1264–1274, Melbourne, Australia. Association for Computational Linguistics.

Longyue Wang, Zhaopeng Tu, Andy Way, and Qun Liu. 2017a. Exploiting cross-sentence context for neural machine translation. In *Proceedings of the 2017 Conference on Empirical Methods in Natural Language Processing*, pages 2826–2831, Copenhagen, Denmark. Association for Computational Linguistics.

Yizhong Wang, Sujian Li, and Houfeng Wang. 2017b. A two-stage parsing method for text-level discourse analysis. In *Proceedings of the 55th Annual Meeting of the Association for Computational Linguistics (Volume 2: Short Papers)*, pages 184–188, Vancouver, Canada. Association for Computational Linguistics.

Yizhong Wang, Sujian Li, and Jingfeng Yang. 2018. Toward fast and accurate neural discourse segmentation. In *Proceedings of the 2018 Conference on*

Empirical Methods in Natural Language Processing, pages 962–967, Brussels, Belgium. Association for Computational Linguistics.

Tong Xiao, Jingbo Zhu, Shujie Yao, and Hao Zhang. 2011. Document-level consistency verification in machine translation. *Proceedings of the 13th Machine Translation Summit*, 13:131–138.

Xinyan Xiao, Deyi Xiong, Min Zhang, Qun Liu, and Shouxun Lin. 2012. A topic similarity model for hierarchical phrase-based translation. In *Proceedings of the 50th Annual Meeting of the Association for Computational Linguistics (Volume 1: Long Papers)*, pages 750–758, Jeju Island, Korea. Association for Computational Linguistics.

Zhengxin Yang, Jinchao Zhang, Fandong Meng, Shuhao Gu, Yang Feng, and Jie Zhou. 2019. Enhancing context modeling with a query-guided capsule network for document-level translation. In *Proceedings of the 2019 Conference on Empirical Methods in Natural Language Processing and the 9th International Joint Conference on Natural Language Processing*, pages 1527–1537, Hong Kong, China. Association for Computational Linguistics.

Zichao Yang, Diyi Yang, Chris Dyer, Xiaodong He, Alex Smola, and Eduard Hovy. 2016. Hierarchical attention networks for document classification. In *Proceedings of the 2016 Conference of the North American Chapter of the Association for Computational Linguistics: Human Language Technologies*, pages 1480–1489, San Diego, California. Association for Computational Linguistics.

Yasuhisa Yoshida, Jun Suzuki, Tsutomu Hirao, and Masaaki Nagata. 2014. Dependency-based discourse parser for single-document summarization. In *Proceedings of the 2014 Conference on Empirical Methods in Natural Language Processing (EMNLP)*, pages 1834–1839, Doha, Qatar. Association for Computational Linguistics.

Biao Zhang, Deyi Xiong, Jinsong Su, Hong Duan, and Min Zhang. 2016. Variational neural machine translation. In *Proceedings of the 2016 Conference on Empirical Methods in Natural Language Processing*, pages 521–530, Austin, Texas. Association for Computational Linguistics.

Jiacheng Zhang, Huanbo Luan, Maosong Sun, Feifei Zhai, Jingfang Xu, Min Zhang, and Yang Liu. 2018. Improving the transformer translation model with document-level context. In *Proceedings of the 2018 Conference on Empirical Methods in Natural Language Processing*, pages 533–542, Brussels, Belgium. Association for Computational Linguistics.

BIT's system for the AutoSimTrans 2020

Minqin Li, Haodong Cheng, Yuanjie Wang, Sijia Zhang
Liting Wu, and **Yuhang Guo***
Beijing Institute of Technology, Beijing, China
lmqminqinli@163.com guoyuhang@bit.edu.cn

Abstract

This paper describes our machine translation systems for the streaming Chinese-to-English translation task of AutoSimTrans 2020. We present a sentence length based method and a sentence boundary detection model based method for the streaming input segmentation. Experimental results of the transcription and the ASR output translation on the development data sets show that the translation system with the detection model based method outperforms the one with the length based method in BLEU score by 1.19 and 0.99 respectively under similar or better latency.

1 Introduction

Automatic simultaneous machine translation is a useful technique in many speech translation scenarios. Compared with traditional machine translations, simultaneous translation focuses on processing streaming inputs of spoken language and achieving low latency translations. Two challenges have to be faced in this task. On one hand, few parallel corpora in spoken language domain are open available, which leads to the fact that the translation performance is not as good as in general domain. On the other hand, traditional machine translation takes a full sentence as input so that the latency of the translation is relatively long.

To deal with the shortage of the spoken language corpora, we pre-train a machine translation model on general domain corpus and then fine-tune this model with limited spoken language corpora. We also augment the spoken language corpora with different strategies to increase the in-domain corpora.

In order to reduce the translation latency, we use three sentence segmentation methods: a punctuation based method, a length based method and a sentence boundary detection model based method. All of the methods can split the input source sentence into short pieces, which makes the translation model obtain low latency translations.

In the streaming automatic speech recognition(ASR) output track for the Chinese-to-English translation task of AutoSimTrans 2020, most of our proposed systems outperform the baseline systems in BLEU score and the sentence boundary detection model based sentence segmentation method abstains higher BLEU score than the length based method under similar latency.

2 Task Description

We participated in the streaming Chinese-to-English translation task of AutoSimTrans 2020 [1]: the streaming ASR output translation track and the streaming transcription translation track. The two tracks are similar except that the ASR output may contain error results and includes no internal punctuation but end punctuation. Table 1 shows an example of the streaming ASR output translation.

3 Approaches

Our all systems can be divided into 3 parts: data preprocessing, sentence segmentation and translation. Data preprocessing includes data cleaning, data augmentation. We implement 3 sentence segmentation methods, which are based on punctuation, sentence length and a sentence boundary detection model. The training of translation model includes pre-training out of domain and fine-tuning in domain.

*Corresponding author.

[1] https://autosimtrans.github.io/shared

Proceedings of the 1st Workshop on Automatic Simultaneous Translation, pages 37–44
July 10, 2020. ©2020 Association for Computational Linguistics

Streaming ASR output	Translation
大 大家 大家好 大家好欢迎	Hello everyone.
大家好欢迎大 大家好欢迎大家	Welcome
大家好欢迎大家来到	everyone
大家好欢迎大家来到这里	to come
大家好欢迎大家来到这里,	here.

Table 1: An example of streaming ASR output translations.

3.1 Data Cleaning

Noises in large-scale parallel corpus are almost inevitable. We clean the parallel corpus for the training. Here we mainly focus on the miss-aligned errors in the training corpus. We find that in the CWMT19 zh-en data set, some of the target sentences are not in English, but in Chinese, Japanese, French or some other noisy form. We suspect these small noises may affect the training of the model. Inspired by Bérard et al. (2019), we apply a language detection script, *langid.py*[2], to the source and the target sentence of the CWMT19 data set separately. Sentence pairs which are not matched with their expected languages are deleted. The corpus are then cleaned by the *tensor2tensor*[3] module by default. Eventually the CWMT19 corpus are then filtered from 9,023,708 pairs into 7,227,510 pairs after data cleaning.

3.2 Data Augmentation

Insufficiency of training data is common in spoken language translation, and many data augmentation methods are used to alleviate this problem (Li et al., 2018). In the streaming ASR output translation system, we use the homophone substitution method to augment the training data according to the characteristics of ASR output translation. The results of ASR usually contain errors of homophonic substitution. We randomly replace each character in the source language part of the training corpus with probability p with its homophones to improve the generalization ability of the system. As shown in Table 2, we find characters that are homophonic with the selected characters, sample them according to the probability that these characters appear in the corpus, and substitute them to the corresponding positions. The data augmentation is only used in our MT model's training because of the insufficiency of training data in spoken language domain.

Similarly, we randomly substitute words in the source language sentences with the homophone substitution. The result of this substitution is closer to the real speech recognition result. As shown in Table 3. We first split the sentence in the source language into a word sequence, determine whether to replace each word with its homophones by probability p, and then sample them according to the distribution of homophones in a corpus. Finally we replace to the corresponding position.

In this system, we adopt the character and the word frequency distribution in an ASR corpus, the AISHELL-2 corpus (Du et al., 2018), and set the substitution probability $p = 0.3$.

3.3 Sentence Segmentation

Low latency is important to simultaneous machine translation. Our systems are closed to low latency translation by splitting long input word sequences into short ones. We use three sentence segmentation methods in this work, namely, punctuation based sentence segmentation (PSS), length based sentence segmentation (LSS), and sentence boundary detection model based sentence segmentation (MSS).

PSS In the punctuation based sentence segmentation method we put the streaming input tokens into a buffer one by one. When the input token is a punctuation, the word sequence in the buffer is translated. Then the buffer is cleared and we put the next tokens into it. The above procedure repeats until the end of the streaming inputs.

LSS In our length based sentence segmentation method we put the steaming input tokens into a buffer one by one. When the input token is a punctuation or the sequence length in the buffer reaches a threshold L, the word sequence in the buffer except the last word is translated in case of the last word is an in complete one. The translated part in the buffer is then cleared and then we put the next tokens

[2]https://github.com/saffsd/langid.py

[3]https://github.com/tensorflow/tensor2tensor

Original Chinese	这个	社 (she)	会	没有	信任	没法	运转
English	This	society	society	hasn't	trust	it doesn't	work
Substitution	这个	设 (she)	会	没有	新人	没法	运转
English	This	suppose	society	hasn't	newcomers	it doesn't	work

Table 2: A randomly selected single character (in red bold font) is substituted by its homophonic character. The corresponding pinyin is included in the bracket.

Original Chinese	这个	社会	没有	信任 (xinren)	没法	运转
English	This	society	hasn't	trust	it doesn't	work
Substitution	这个	社会	没有	新人 (xinren)	没法	运转
English	This	society	hasn't	newcomers	it doesn't	work

Table 3: A randomly selected word (in red bold font) is substituted by its homophonic word. The corresponding pinyin is included in the bracket.

into the buffer. The above procedure repeats until the end of the streaming inputs.

Text	Label
所以我们认为免费 So we think that free	0
所以我们认为免费只是暂时的 So we think that free is only temporary	1

Table 4: Examples of the train data set of the model. 1: Complete sentences. 0: Incomplete sentence.

MSS Apparently many translation inputs with the LSS are incomplete sentences fragments because of the "hard" sentence segmentation. Here we propose a sentence boundary detection model for the sentence segmentation. We build this model on the top of a pretraining model, BERT(Devlin et al., 2018). Our model is built by adding two layers of full connected network to the Chinese BERT pre-training model. The training data set is constructed using all transcription pairs provided by the organizer. For the sentences in transcriptions, we use a punctuation set, {, . ! ? }, as the sentence boundary indicators to obtain complete sentences, which are used as positive samples. And then we sample incomplete fragments from the above sentences uniformly to obtain negative samples. The ratio of the positive sample to the negative sample is 1 : 4. Table 4 illustrates a positive example and a negative example. The training set is of 370k examples, the test set is of 7k examples, and the validation set is of 7k examples. After running 3 epochs, the model converges with an accuracy of 92.5% in the test set.

We apply the sentence boundary detection model to streaming ASR output translation. The model returns the prediction to each streaming sequence as a judgment condition for whether it is to be translated. However, we should not set the segmentation point at the first position of the detection. Suppose a detected sentence boundary position is i and the next detected boundary position is $i+1$. This means both of the prefix word sequences $w_{1:i}$ and $w_{1:i+1}$ can be seen as a complete sentence. Usually the boundary position $i+1$ is better than i. Generally we set a rule that position i is a sentence boundary if the sentence boundary detection model returns true for position i and false for $i+1$. In this way, the word sequence (i.e. $w_{1:i}$) is feed to the translation system when it is detected and the untranslated part (i.e. w_{i+1}) will be translated in the next sentence. For example, the position i of streaming inputs in Table 5 are detected to boundary's position finally only when the position i is detected to boundary by model while the next position $i+1$ isn't detected to boundary by model.

3.4 Pre-training and Fine-tuning

Pre-training and fine-tuning are the most popular training methods in the field of deep learning. It has been proved that this training mode is very effective in improving the performance of the model and is very simple to implement. Therefore, we use the CWMT19

Position	Sentence	Return of model	Boundary
$i-2$	她喜欢那个公司的设	False	0
$i-1$	她喜欢那个公司的设计	True	0
i	她喜欢那个公司的设计师	True	1
$i+1$	她喜欢那个公司的设计师因	False	0

Table 5: The examples of using model to detect boundaries. 0: Not boundary of sentence, 1: Boundary of sentence

data set to pre-train a base-model, and then use the speech translation data provided by the organizer to fine-tune the model.

We first train a basic Transformer translation model with CWMT19 data set. In order to adapt to the spoken language domain, we directly fine-tune the pre-trained model on the transcriptions or ASR outputs provided by the organizer and our augmented data.

4 Experiments

4.1 Data Sets

Data Set	# Sentence Pairs
CWMT19	9,023,708
Transcriptions	37,901
ASR Outputs	202,237
Development Set	956

Table 6: The size of different data sets.

We train our model with the CWMT19 zh-en data set, the streaming transcription and the streaming ASR output data sets provided by the evaluation organizer. Because of the evaluation track limit, we did not use the UN parallel corpus and the News Commentary corpus although they were used in the baseline. The CWMT19 zh-en data set includes six sub data sets: the casia2015 corpus, the casict2011 corpus, the casict2015 corpus, the datum2015 corpus, the datum2017 corpus and the neu2017 corpus. The CWMT19 data set contains totally 9,023,708 parallel sentences. They are used in the pre-training of our model. Streaming transcription and streaming ASR output data sets are provided by the evaluation organizer. The transcription data set contains 37,901 pairs and the ASR output data set contains 202,237 pairs. We use them as the fine-tuning data to adapt to the spoken language. Finally we evaluate our system on the development set which contains 956 pairs. The size of the data set is listed in Table 6.

4.2 System Settings

Our model is based on the transformer in *tensor2tensor*. We set the parameters of the model as $transformer\_big$. And we set the parameter *problem* as *translate_enzh_wmt32k_rev*. We train the model on 6 RTX-Titan GPUs for 9 days. Then we use the transcription data and the ASR output data to fine-tune the model respectively on 2 GPUs. We fine-tune the model until it overfits.

4.3 Baseline Model

The baseline model[4] (Ma et al., 2018) provided by the evaluation organizer is trained on the WMT18 zh-en data set, including CWMT19, the UN parallel corpus, and the News Commentary corpus. The baseline model uses the transformer which is essentially the same as the base model from the original paper (Vaswani et al., 2017). It applied a Prefix-to-Prefix architecture and Wait-K strategy to the transformer. We test the Wait-1, Wait-3 and the FULL model with fine-tuning on domain data as the comparison to our system. For the Wait-1, Wait-3 setting, the baseline fine-tunes 30,000 steps. For the FULL setting, the baseline fine-tunes 40,000 steps.

4.4 Latency Metric: Average Lagging

Ma et al. (2018) uses Average Lagging (AL) as the latency metric. They defined:

$$\mathrm{AL}_g(\mathbf{x},\mathbf{y}) = \frac{1}{\tau_g(|\mathbf{x}|)} \sum_{t=1}^{\tau_g(|\mathbf{x}|)} g(t) - \frac{t-1}{r} \quad (1)$$

Where $\tau_g(|\mathbf{x}|)$ denotes the cut-off step which is the decoding step when source sentence finishes, $g(t)$ denotes the number of source words

[4]https://github.com/autosimtrans/SimulTransBaseline

processed by the encoder when deciding the target word $\mathbf{y}_t$, and $r = |x|/|y|$ is the target-to-source length ratio. The lower the AL value, the lower the delay, the better the real-time system.

5 Results

5.1 Streaming Transcription Translation

The results of our streaming transcription system on the development data set are shown in Table 7. FT-Trans indicates the fine-tuning data set including the original transcriptions and the transcriptions without punctuation (i.e. the depunctuation version). LSS-L indicates the system with the length based sentence segmentation method and the threshold for the length is L. PSS indicates the system with our punctuation based sentence segmentation method. MSS indicates the system with our sentence boundary detection model based sentence segmentation method. Wait-1, Wait-3 and FULL indicate the different settings of the baseline systems. Among these settings, the best AL score is from the Wait-1 baseline and the best BLEU score is from our PSS system. Under similar BLEU score, LSS-17 obtains better AL score than the FULL baseline. Both of the AL and the BLEU score of the LSS-L system grow up with L increases. The MSS system performs better BLEU score by 1.19 than the LSS-L system under similar AL score (i.e. MSS vs. LSS-12).

Finally we submitted the PSS setting system because of its high BLEU score and relatively low AL latency compared with the FULL baseline.

5.2 Streaming ASR Output Translation

The translation performances on the streaming ASR output are shown in Table 8. FT-ASR represents the systems are fine-tuned on the combination of the ASR output and the ASR output without punctuation. FT-ASR+Aug represents the fine-tuning set includes the FT-ASR, the homophone substitution augmented transcriptions, and their depunctuation version. FT-ASR+Aug+Trans represents the fine-tuning set contains the FT-ASR+Aug and the transcriptions and their

Models	Settings	AL	BLEU
FT-Trans	LSS-10	5.9273	17.31
	LSS-11	6.3180	18.12
	LSS-12	6.6932	18.36
	LSS-15	7.7651	20.71
	LSS-17	8.2813	21.84
	PSS	**10.0667**	**24.23**
	MSS	6.7249	19.55
Baseline	Wait-1	2.1014	15.07
	Wait-3	5.1424	17.95
	FULL	24.9331	21.65

Table 7: The translation results on the development data set of streaming transcriptions.

depunctuation version.

As shown in Table 8, all of our systems outperform the Wait-1, Wait-3 settings of the baseline in BLEU score and our MSS model outperforms the FULL baseline. As more data is added to the fine-tuning set, the performances of the systems will increase accordingly. Both LSS-15 and PSS in FT-ASR+Aug outperform the corresponding systems in FT-ASR, which indicates the effectiveness of the data augmentation. The BLEU score of LSS-15(FT-ASR+Aug+Trans) is 2.22 higher than LSS-15(FT-ASR) while the AL latency of former is better than the latter.

In the FT-ASR+Aug+Trans, the sentence boundary detection model based sentence segmentation, MSS, obtains higher (i.e. +0.99) BLEU score and lower (i.e. -1.06) AL latency than the LSS-15. The BLEU score of MSS is lower than PSS by 1.46 but the latency is improved by 15.88.

Compared with the results of transcription translation of FT-Trans in Table 7, the BLEU scores of the ASR outputs translations relatively decreased. This indicates the effects of the cascade error of the ASR systems.

The latency of the LSS in Table 7 and Table 8 are close. The latency of PSS increased from 10 to around 22. This indicates the lack of punctuation in the ASR outputs.

The MSS system performs close AL latency and less BLEU score drops in transcription and ASR outputs translation. At last we submitted the MSS system to the evaluation track.

Several examples of the translation in differ-

Models	Settings	AL	BLEU
FT-ASR	LSS-15	7.5636	13.62
	PSS	22.0051	18.23
FT-ASR	LSS-15	7.2222	14.99
+Aug	PSS	21.9600	18.29
FT-ASR	LSS-15	7.1298	15.84
+Aug	PSS	21.9557	18.29
+Trans	**MSS**	**6.0709**	**16.83**
Baseline	Wait-1	1.0766	10.72
	Wait-3	3.9692	12.75
	FULL	24.0415	15.13

Table 8: The translation results on the development data set of streaming ASR outputs.

ent systems can be seen in Appendix A.

6 Related Work

End-to-end machine translation models, such as transformer (Vaswani et al., 2017), greatly promote the progress of machine translation research and have been applied to speech translation researches (Schneider and Waibel, 2019; Srinivasan et al., 2019; Wetesko et al., 2019). Furthermore, several end-to-end based approaches have recently been proposed for simultaneous translations (Zheng et al., 2019b,a).

In order to solve the problem of insufficient parallel corpus data for simultaneous translation tasks, Schneider and Waibel (2019) augmented the available training data using back-translation. Vial et al. (2019) used BERT pre-training model to train a large number of external monolingual data to achieve data augmentation. Li et al. (2018) simulated the input noise of ASR model and used placeholders, homophones and high-frequency words to replace the original parallel corpus at the character level. Inspired by Li et al. (2018), we augment the training data by randomly replacing the words in the source sentences with homophones.

In order to reduce the translation latency, Ma et al. (2018) used the Prefix-to-Prefix architecture, which predicts the target word with the prefix rather than the whole sequence. Their Wait-K models are used as the baseline and are provided by the shared task organizers. The Wait-K models start to predict the target after the first K source words appear. Zheng et al. (2020) applied ensemble of models trained with a set of Wait-K polices to achieve an adaptive policy. Xiong et al. (2019) have proposed a pre-training based segmentation method which is similar to MSS. However, in the decoding stage, the time complex of this method is $O(n^2)$ whereas the time complex of MSS is $O(n)$.

7 Conclusions

In this paper, we describe our submission systems to the the streaming Chinese-to-English translation task of AutoSimTrans 2020. In this system the translation model is trained on the CWMT19 data set with the transformer modedalvi2018incrementall. We leverage homophonic character and word substitutions to augment the fine-tuning speech transcription data set. We implement a punctuation based, a length based and a sentence boundary detection model based sentence segmentation methods to improve the latency of the translation system. Experimental results on the development data sets show that the punctuation based sentence segmentation obtains the best BLEU score with a reasonable latency on the transcription translation track. The results on the ASR outputs translation show the effectiveness of our data augmentation approaches. And the sentence boundary detection model based sentence segmentation gives the low latency and a stable BLEU score in our all systems. However, because we have no enough time to retrain the MT model, some settings of our system are not consistent with the baseline, so it is difficult to judge whether our method is better than baseline's method. In the future, we will finish this comparative experiment.

Acknowledgments

Supported by the National Key Research and Development Program of China (No. 2016YFB0801200)

References

Alexandre Bérard, Ioan Calapodescu, and Claude Roux. 2019. Naver labs europe's systems for the wmt19 machine translation robustness task. *arXiv preprint arXiv:1907.06488*.

Jacob Devlin, Ming-Wei Chang, Kenton Lee, and Kristina Toutanova. 2018. BERT: pre-training of deep bidirectional transformers for language understanding. *CoRR*, abs/1810.04805.

Jiayu Du, Xingyu Na, Xuechen Liu, and Hui Bu. 2018. AISHELL-2: transforming mandarin ASR research into industrial scale. *CoRR*, abs/1808.10583.

Xiang Li, Haiyang Xue, Wei Chen, Yang Liu, Yang Feng, and Qun Liu. 2018. Improving the robustness of speech translation. *arXiv preprint arXiv:1811.00728*.

Mingbo Ma, Liang Huang, Hao Xiong, Kaibo Liu, Chuanqiang Zhang, Zhongjun He, Hairong Liu, Xing Li, and Haifeng Wang. 2018. STACL: simultaneous translation with integrated anticipation and controllable latency. *CoRR*, abs/1810.08398.

Felix Schneider and Alex Waibel. 2019. Kit' s submission to the iwslt 2019 shared task on text translation. In *Proceedings of the 16th International Workshop on Spoken Language Translation*.

Tejas Srinivasan, Ramon Sanabria, and Florian Metze. 2019. Cmu' s machine translation system for iwslt 2019.

Ashish Vaswani, Noam Shazeer, Niki Parmar, Jakob Uszkoreit, Llion Jones, Aidan N. Gomez, Lukasz Kaiser, and Illia Polosukhin. 2017. Attention is all you need. *CoRR*, abs/1706.03762.

Loïc Vial, Benjamin Lecouteux, Didier Schwab, Hang Le, and Laurent Besacier. 2019. The lig system for the english-czech text translation task of iwslt 2019.

Joanna Wetesko, Marcin Chochowski, Pawel Przybysz, Philip Williams, Roman Grundkiewicz, Rico Sennrich, Barry Haddow, Antonio Valerio Miceli Barone, and Alexandra Birch. 2019. Samsung and university of edinburgh' s system for the iwslt 2019.

Hao Xiong, Ruiqing Zhang, Chuanqiang Zhang, Zhongjun He, Hua Wu, and Haifeng Wang. 2019. Dutongchuan: Context-aware translation model for simultaneous interpreting. *arXiv preprint arXiv:1907.12984*.

Baigong Zheng, Kaibo Liu, Renjie Zheng, Mingbo Ma, Hairong Liu, and Liang Huang. 2020. Simultaneous translation policies: From fixed to adaptive.

Baigong Zheng, Renjie Zheng, Mingbo Ma, and Liang Huang. 2019a. Simpler and faster learning of adaptive policies for simultaneous translation. *arXiv preprint arXiv:1909.01559*.

Baigong Zheng, Renjie Zheng, Mingbo Ma, and Liang Huang. 2019b. Simultaneous translation with flexible policy via restricted imitation learning. In *Proceedings of the 57th Annual Meeting of the Association for Computational Linguistics*, pages 5816–5822, Florence, Italy. Association for Computational Linguistics.

A Appendices

We list several translation results to compare our systems with the baselines on the transcription translation track and the ASR output translation track. As shown in Table 9 and 10, missing translation can be observed in the Wait-K baselines and our system.

Source	Reference
在他每一次比赛都是输，甚至是倒数第一第二名的时候，是什么，是什么样的力量支撑着他一直去比赛，一直去训练。	He has always been ranked among the last, so to speak, the last in those games. What kind of spirit supported him to take part in the competition all the time?

Table 9: An example of source sentence and reference translation in the transcription translation track.

For streaming ASR output, as shown in Table 12, missing translation can also be observed in the Wait-K baselines. From Table 13, we can see that in the segmentation of the LSS-15 most of the sentence fragments are incomplete. As shown in Table 14, the segmentation of the MSS is reasonable and the translation is much better than the LSS-15.

System	Translation
Wait-1	In his every after shock, he won the game, even in the No.1 games.
Wait-3	Every time when he does a match, he will lose, even in the No.1 draw, what is that?
FULL	In every game, which is not only about the win, but also about the power that comes to the 1st place, those who support him to go on training all the time.
FT-Trans(PSS)	In every game he lost, in the second countdown, what is it? What was the strength that kept him going? I keep training.

Table 10: The translations of the sentence in Table 9.

Source	Reference
对吗每个人都是不想输的都是想赢的在它每一次比赛都是输甚至是倒数第第二名的时候什么是什么样的力量支撑着他一直去比赛	Right? Everyone does not want to lose; rather, they all want to win.When he lost every match or even came in the second last or last place, what was it or what kind of strength supported him to compete and train all the time?

Table 11: An example of the source sentence and the reference translation in the ASR output translation track.

System	Translation
Wait-1	So, is everyone wants to fail?
Wait-3	Right, everyone never want to fail, and they all want to win every game, even when they are in the second best.
FULL	That is, to say, every one would never want to win, in every game, or even in the second place, what was the power that supports him to go there and that number?

Table 12: The translations of the sentence in Table 11.

Segmentation	Translation
对吗每个人都是不想输的都是想	Yes, everyone wants to lose.
赢的在它每一次比赛都是输甚至	The winner lost every game.
是倒数第第二名的时候什么是	What is second to last?
什么样的力量支撑着他一直去	What kind of strength supports him to go on?
比赛	The game.

Table 13: The sentence segmentation and the corresponding translations in Table 11 with the setting of LSS-15 on FT-ASR+Aug+Trans.

Segmentation	Translation
对吗每个人都是不想输的	Right? Everyone doesn't want to lose.
都是想赢的	They all want to win.
在它每一次比赛都是输甚至是倒数	In each game, it is losing or even losing.
第第二名的时候	In the second place.
什么是什么样的力量	What is power?
支撑着他一直去比赛	It supports him to go all the way to the game.

Table 14: The sentence segmentation and the corresponding translations in Table 11 with the setting of MSS on FT-ASR+Aug+Trans.

Author Index

Association for Computational Linguistics
209 N. Eighth Street
Stroudsburg, Pennsylvania 18360

ISBN 978-1-7138-1391-0

CURRAN ASSOCIATES INC.
proceedings.com